BOATHOUSES

ADAM MORNEMENT
BOATHOUSES

F

FRANCES LINCOLN LIMITED

PUBLISHERS

CONTENTS

INTRODUCTION   **6**

EIGHTEENTH CENTURY   **32**

Botny domik, Peter-Paul Fortress, St Petersburg, Russia 34 | Traditional South Sea Boathouses, Society Islands (French Polynesia), South Pacific 36 | Fishing Room and Boathouse, Kedleston Hall, Derbyshire, England 40

NINETEENTH CENTURY   **44**

Obersee Boathouse, Berchtesgaden National Park, Bavaria, Germany 46 | Greenway Boathouse, Devon, England 48 | The Dylan Thomas Boathouse, Laugharne, Carmarthenshire, Wales 50 | Scotney Castle Boathouse, Kent, England 52 | Wray Castle Boathouse, Ambleside, Cumbria, England 54 | Haslar Gunboat Yard, Gosport, Hampshire, England 56 | Sheerness Boatstore, Kent, England 58 | Victorian Boathouse, Trevarno, Cornwall, England 60 | Duke of Portland Boathouse, Ullswater, Cumbria, England 64 | The Boathouses of Tigre, Paraná Delta, Argentina 66 | Boathouse Row, Philadelphia, Pennsylvania, USA 70 | Walmer Lifeboat Station, Kent, England 72 | Reale Societa Canottieri Cerea, Turin, Italy 76 | Lodge Park Sherbourne Estate, Gloucestershire, England 78 | Clovelly Lifeboat Station, Devon, England 82

TWENTIETH CENTURY   **84**

Ryoan-ji Boathouse, Kyoto, Japan 86 | Frank Lloyd Wright's Fontana Boathouse, Buffalo, New York, USA 88 | Humboldt Park Boathouse, Chicago, USA 92 | Queenscliff Lifeboat Station, Victoria, Australia 96 | Noah's Boathouse, Buckinghamshire, England 98 | Oxford University Boathouses, Oxford, England 100 | Carmel College, Wallingford, Berkshire, England 106 | Maori waka and korowai, Waitangi, New Zealand 110 | Arc, shelter for Alvar Aalto's boat, Muuratsalo, Finland 114 | Northbridge Boathouse, Sydney, Australia 118

TWENTY-FIRST CENTURY   **118**

Fussach Bootshaus, Vorarlberg, Austria 120 | Lake Austin Boat Dock, Texas, USA 124 | Minneapolis Rowing Club, USA 128 | Muskoka Boathouse, Ontario, Canada 132 | Maritime Youth House, Copenhagen, Denmark 138 | Centre d'Interpretation du Canal, Pouilly-en-Auxois, France 142 | Porter Boathouse, University of Wisconsin, USA 146 | Tenby Lifeboat Station, Pembrokeshire, Wales 148 | Plinio Torno Sports Club, Lake Como, Italy 152 | Chesapeake Boathouse, Oklahoma, USA 156 | *Luna Rossa* Team Base, Valencia, Spain 160 | Floating Boathouse, Lake Huron, Ontario, Canada 164 | Louise-Catherine, Paris, France 168

Bibliography | Acknowledgements   172
Picture credits   173
Index   174

INTRODUCTION

The boathouse is an ancient building type. For thousands of years, communities living beside lakes, rivers and seas have built enclosures to construct and protect a life-giving means of trade and communication, particularly in locations prone to climatic extremes. But examples of ancient boathouses are rare.

The vast majority of boathouses are humble, utilitarian structures erected for a specific purpose. They are generally ephemeral buildings, with improvised frames sheathed in low-cost materials. Most are subject to regular modification.

Repairing and rebuilding a boathouse, whether replacing decayed fabric or shoring up waterlogged footings, is an essential part of the maintenance and construction process. This is partly the consequence of exposure to saline conditions and fierce weather, and partly because of the prime importance of their locations. Good sites for boathouses – those that are sheltered, secure and accessible from land and water – are few and far between. They are also often in sensitive locations: in many parts of the world severe restrictions are imposed on the development of previously untouched sites next to the water's edge, in order to minimise erosion and protect breeding grounds. These are some of the reasons why the sites of boathouses often endure much longer than the original boathouses.

Documentary evidence of the recycling of boathouse sites is hard to come by, ephemeral structures rarely being recorded before the invention of photography. One example is revealed in *Halsnøy Kloster*, a 1656 landscape by Norwegian Elias Fiigenschough. It depicts the partially ruined Halsnøy Monastery, following the Norwegian reformation of 1537. The monastery

TITLE PAGE | Boat sheds at Robinson's Bay, Akaroa Harbour, New Zealand.

CONTENTS PAGE | A yellow-painted timber boathouse at Hafrsfjord, Norway. Boats are hung from davits inside the superstructure, raising them above frozen water during the winter.

PREVIOUS PAGE | Timber boathouse at the end of a timber jetty on Amersee, Bavaria, Germany.

LEFT | Silhouette of boathouse at Hoopers Bay, near Dunedin, South Island, New Zealand.

LEFT | *Halsnøy Kloster*, a 1656 landscape by Norwegian painter Elias Fiigenschough. The building in the centre foreground is a boathouse built of local timber with a stave construction frame.

BELOW | The Halsnøy Monastery boathouse pictured in 2008. The framing system and location of the boathouse are unchanged since at least the mid-1600s.

occupies a narrow neck of land on a windswept Norwegian island. It was founded by Viking chief Erling Skakke (Erling the Wry) in 1164, although human settlement dates back much further; the remains of a boat dating to at least 300BC were found in a nearby peat bog in 1896.

Two buildings in the foreground of the painting define Klostervågen, a small harbour: a store to the right, and a boathouse to the left. The boathouse is still standing today, its fabric upgraded, but its form, location and stave construction essentially unchanged since the mid-1600s, probably much earlier.

Other examples of contemporary boathouses on established sites include the Duke of Portland Boathouse on Ullswater, a Victorian structure whose foundations date to at least the seventeenth century (see pages 64–65); the simple bamboo shelter at Ryoan-ji Temple in Kyoto (see page 13); and the timber *bootshaus* on the east shore of Obersee in Bavaria (see pages 46–47).

ABOVE | Houses with integrated wet docks line the shore of Ine, a Japanese fishing village.

BELOW LEFT | 'A jolly place to loaf': Two-storey timber boathouse built by American yacht designer and photographer Ralph M Munrow on Biscayne Bay, Florida in 1887, pictured during the 1920s.

BELOW | The first floor of Ralph Munroe's timber boathouse, possibly with Munroe seated, pictured during the 1920s.

Diversity

Since the late-eighteenth century, the nature and scale of boathouses has changed. Advances in construction technology, dramatic urban expansion, investment in defence fleets, the evolution of rowing as a social and sporting activity and improved methods for aiding vessels in distress are just some of the factors that have increased the variety of boathouses.

The examples presented in this volume are a broad cross section of types and varieties of boathouses built in sixteen countries since the mid-eighteenth century. They include ceremonial boathouses, boathouses serving as mausoleums or as eye catchers in the landscape, boathouses in public parks or built for rowing clubs, military facilities, lifeboat stations and private writing rooms. Some are the work of famous architects; others are anonymous. Each in its own way embodies the adventure, charm and romance that characterize this ancient, global but all-too-often overlooked building type.

BELOW | A terrace of timber-framed boathouses on the Japanese island of Oki houses the local fishing fleet.

PREVIOUS PAGE | Stone boathouse with integrated wet dock at Devoke Water, Lake District, Cumbria, England.

LEFT | An unidentified Lake District boathouse and jetty, pictured in 1958.

ABOVE | Boathouse at Wroxham Broad, East Anglia, England, late-nineteenth century. This type of low-cost boathouse, once common in East Anglia, was formed by enclosing a timber frame with reed walls held in place by deal battens. The roof was either tiled or thatched.

Landscape gardens (1750s–1830s)

Like most building types, the appearance, siting, even the practical function of boathouses has been influenced by social, aesthetic and economic trends. In Georgian England, for instance, the boathouse played a minor role in the landscape garden style popularised by the prolific Lancelot 'Capability' Brown (1716–83) from the 1750s, and taken up later by Humphry Repton, John Nash and the Victorian park makers.

The English landscape garden rejected formality, with its straight avenues, clipped hedges and shaped trees, in favour of a romantic approach that revealed and accentuated the natural beauty of the landscape. The idea was that visitors to landscape gardens would stroll or ride along gently curving paths, alongside serpentine streams and through woods and meadows, stopping occasionally to admire unexpected vistas including eye-catching features like a miniature Italian temple or Gothic gazebo.

The range of possibilities in an English landscape garden was enormous: trees and shrubs of all colours and textures mingled to create a great sense of the unexpected, and boathouses were a useful and attractive addition to the scene. They were popular features in gardens that featured lakes. Stourhead in Wiltshire is a prime example. The garden is arranged around a large manmade lake. On the anti-clockwise route around the lake, the eye is drawn to a range of temples, grottoes and follies, in an array of styles. The grotto-style boathouse, near the Temple of Flora on the east side of the lake, was added in the 1790s.

A later example is at Woodchester, near Stroud in Gloucestershire. 'Capability' Brown and his assistant John Speyers had visited Woodchester Park in 1782, but no landscaping work was carried out, possibly due to Brown's death in 1783. In 1809, Humphry Repton was consulted about the beautification of the grounds, following which a chain of lakes was established. In the 1830s his architect son John Adey Repton was commissioned to oversee alterations to the main house, and the construction of a picturesque two-storey boathouse on one of the lakes.

The influence of the English landscape style was enormous. English country squires aspired to have their house set in a landscaped park, planting 'belts' of trees to screen unwanted

RIGHT | The two-storey stone-built boathouse at Woodchester Park, Gloucestershire, England, was built during works to beautify the estate in the 1830s.

vistas, and creating paths to lead visitors in the desired direction (see also Kedleston, pages 40–43). Industrialists also saw the merit of beautifying industrial landscapes. Josiah Wedgwood tried to ensure that the Trent and Mersey Canal flowing past Etruria looked like a serpentine river. The influence also extended beyond the British Isles, notably to Russia and Germany.

Urban boathouses (1850s–1920s)

From the mid-nineteenth century, boathouses migrated to the expanding metropolitan centres. Industrial growth spawned disease and sickly pollution. Governments and municipal authorities in Britain, mainland Europe, America and elsewhere responded by building civic parks as places for the masses to take the air. If the park included a water feature, and many did,

public boating was promoted as a healthy pastime, and of course the boats needed to be stored.

Once again, the British influence on this trend was marked. English landscape architect Calvert Vaux designed the first boathouse in Central Park, New York. Boating had been a popular pursuit on the lake in Central Park since the early 1860s. In 1870, Vaux – who invited Frederick Law Olmstead to work with him in preparing a plan for the park in the early-1850s – proposed the construction of a permanent boathouse to replace the series of exposed landing stages around the lake. Vaux designed a two-storey timber-structure with gothic details south of Bethesda Terrace. Completed in 1873, it featured a boat dock below a lake-facing terrace. Vaux's boathouse served the public for 80 years. It was replaced in 1954, by a neo-classical

BELOW | Melbourne, a landscape by Laurence Wilson painted in 1905. There has been a string of boathouses on the south bank of the Yarra since the 1860s.

OVERLEAF | View of Central Park in 1875. Bethesda Terrace is in the centre of the image. The boathouse, designed by Calvert Vaux, is in the centre left, with boat rental facilities on the ground floor and a terrace cafe above.

brick structure named the Loeb Boathouse (named for investment banker and philanthropist Carl M Loeb, who contributed to the costs). (See also Humboldt Park boathouse, Chicago, pages 92–95).

In 1882, a boathouse was added to the Englischer Garten in Munich, a *volkspark* (people's park) inspired by the English landscape garden style. At various stages since it was established in 1789 the Englischer Garten has included farms, nurseries, a sheepfold and an agricultural school, all for the education and enjoyment of urban Bavarians. The boathouse, on the Kleinhesselohe See, the largest of the park's many lakes, provided facilities for relaxation and boat hire. The present boathouse, the third at the Englischer Garten, dates to the mid-1980s.

From the late-nineteenth century, the connection between health and rowing also extended to corporate paternalism. In 1907, Peter Behrens (1868–1940), an artist turned self-trained architect who was a significant influence on the pioneers of the Modern Movement, was appointed artistic consultant to Allgemeine Elektrizitäts-Gesellschaft (AEG), a corporation in the electrical industry. He came to control almost every visual manifestation of the company's identity, including the design of products, graphics and exhibitions, and architecture. The building for which he is arguably best known is the AEG *Turbinehalle* (turbine hall) in Berlin, regarded as an early landmark of modern functional architecture in the machine age. Less well documented is that Behrens designed two boathouses for AEG.

21

The years leading up to World War I were a period of expansion for AEG. Between 1910 and 1915, the company established a complex of factories at Hennigsdorf, about 10 miles/15 kilometres northwest of Berlin. They included facilities for the production of oilcloth, porcelain and varnish, all products related to the electrical industry. At the time Hennigsdorf was largely undeveloped, so AEG tasked Behrens with the design of housing and related facilities for workers, including a small boathouse (since demolished). A larger boathouse, also designed by Behrens, survives at Oberschöneweide, southeast of Berlin on the banks of the River Spree. As originally built, in 1910-11, it comprised boat storage facilities, a dining room, changing room and dormitories for members. Although not among Behrens'

most renowned buildings, the Oberschöneweide boathouse is a substantial structure whose restrained unpretentious form and simply expressed machine-made materials – including red brick, timber shingles and terracotta tiles – reflect Behrens' interest in applying values of craftsmanship in the modern world. It was built for the Elektra Rowing Club, whose members were drawn from AEG's engineering and sales staff.

In cities well integrated with their rivers, there is quite a tradition of groups of boathouses becoming a collective civic landmark. Philadelphia's Boathouse Row is generally regarded as the trendsetter in this sporadic global phenomenon (see pages 70–71). The earliest of the ten boathouses that line the east bank of the Schuylkill River date from the 1870s. They

LEFT | No. 6 Boathouse (built 1846), seen across the Boat Pond at Portsmouth Royal Naval Yard in 1957. The three doorways provided access for boats. The late-nineteenth-century wooden building over the pond on the right, also a boathouse, was typical of timber structures at the Naval Yard.

RIGHT | Three giant shipbuilding slipways enclosed in corrugated iron were built at Deptford Docks, London in 1845-46.

replaced a number of improvised structures which had served the rowers, swimmers and skaters (during winter) who frequented Fairmount Park after 1822, when the completion of the Fairmount Water Works and Dam transformed the Schuylkill from a tidal stream to a long freshwater lake. Boathouse Row was nominated to America's National Register of Historic Places in 1987.

Another 'boathouse row' with nineteenth-century origins is in Melbourne. Boat building workshops and rowing club boathouses have populated the south bank of the Yarra, adjacent to the city centre since the 1860s. By 1911 it was home to a string of eight boathouses designed in a variety of Victorian and Edwardian styles, including the Melbourne Boat Club, Mercantile Rowing Club and the Melbourne University Boat Club. The present generation of boathouses, sandwiched between the Yarra and the Botanic Gardens, all date to the twentieth century.

Today, the city of Oklahoma is developing its own 'boathouse row' as part of a bid to better integrate Oklahoma River with the city. Since the 2006 completion of the Chesapeake Boathouse, a popular rowing facility developed and managed by a not-for-profit organization (see pages 156–159), permission has been granted for the construction of boathouses for Oklahoma City University, the University of Oklahoma and the University of Central Oklahoma, echoing the nineteenth-century pattern of collegiate-led developments. When complete, these boathouses will form a central component of a bid to unify the north and south of Oklahoma City through the revival of its under-developed central river corridor.

Defence

Defence and military endeavour have been the driving forces behind some of the most expensive and technologically advanced boathouses ever built. In almost every instance, they are the product of a government investment.

In 1605, Danish master builder Joseph Matzen was contracted to build a secret enclosed boathouse (or *Galejhus*, galley house) as part of King Christian IV's great armoury complex in Copenhagen. The idea was that the king's fleet, and the cargoes that it carried, could be hidden there, away from the eyes of spies. The Royal Boathouse survives today as the Danish Museum; the conversion was carried out by architect Daniel Libeskind (2003).

The primary motivating force behind the construction of a series of colossal enclosed boat slips by the British Admiralty between the 1830s and 1850s was dry rot, although secrecy and protecting the boat builders from the elements may also have been factors. Traditionally, timber warships had been built in the open air. By the early nineteenth century, the scale and complexity of the vessels meant that they were prone to decay during the long construction process. The problem was that until the 1830s there was no construction material sufficiently lightweight, strong and affordable to enclose the roof spans – timber, slate and stone were all impractical and expensive. The solution to the problem was corrugated iron, a material invented in 1829. Sheets of curved corrugated metal could be fixed end to end to form vaulted roofs with minimal support. The material could also enclose the sides. During the 1830s and 1840s, the British

Admiralty invested heavily in slips at the Royal Dockyards in Chatham, Pembroke, Deptford, Woolwich and Portsmouth. At the time they were some of the largest structures ever built, comparable to cathedrals in volume.

The concept of state-sponsored boathouses for military operations resurfaced during World War II on a grand scale. Following Germany's occupation of Norway, France and the Low Countries in 1940, the Nazis sought to use their fleet of U-boats to control the Atlantic and North Sea shipping lanes. From 1941, vast submarine pens and bunkers were constructed along the Norwegian and French coastlines, at Bergen and Trondheim in Norway, and Brest, Lorient, Saint-Nazaire, La Pallice and Bordeaux in France. Manufacturing and storage facilities for U-boats were also constructed on the German Baltic coast. Depending on local requirements, these colossal complexes of reinforced concrete were equipped with wet and dry docks with construction and maintenance facilities. The Keroman Submarine Base at Lorient was among the more extensive. It

was composed of three interlinked buildings dedicated to a specific function, each with a reinforced concrete roof, seven feet (over 2m) thick, intended to withstand aerial bombardment.

Given their strength and proportions it is little surprise that most of the Nazi U-boat pens survive in some form. Some have been adapted to local naval requirements, others are tourist attractions; one has even been turned into a business park.

Lifeboat stations

Lifeboat stations, located on treacherous and exposed stretches of coastline, are some of the world's most heroic and in some cases enduring boathouses.

The tradition of designing lifeboats, and structures to house them, dates to the early eighteenth century, when committees were formed in towns in France and England to oversee the organized rescue of shipwreck survivors. This activity reached a crescendo towards the beginning of the nineteenth century, a time when approximately a third of British seamen perished

LEFT | Crew members at Gravelines lifeboat station on the French north coast (undated).

BELOW | The boathouse at the French port of Erquy was built into the cliff face. Both the boathouse and the slipway were completed in 1935, to designs by architect Jean Gagey.

either from accidents at sea or in shipwrecks. This chronic loss of life led to the design of novel life-saving devices, including Manby's mortar, which involved firing a shot-weighted rope to wrecked boats, and self-righting vessels that could be launched regardless of weather and circumstance. The loss of life also led, in 1824, to the foundation of the National Institution for the Preservation of Life from Shipwreck, more commonly known as the Shipwreck Institution (from 1854 the Royal National Lifeboat Institution, RNLI). The Institution, a voluntary organization dependent upon donations and subscriptions for funds, was the first of its type in the world. Today there are equivalents in seafaring nations the world over, including France, Germany, Holland, Sweden, South Africa, the USA, New Zealand, Australia and China.

The RNLI got off to a good start; in 1824/25, £10,000 was generated in donations and subscriptions. But things quickly

faltered; by 1832/33, donations were down to only £254. The situation picked up in 1850, with the appointment of the Duke of Northumberland as President of the Institution (a position that had never previously been occupied). The following year the duke announced a competition for the best model of a lifeboat at the 1851 Great Exhibition. Buoyancy and the stability of boats were primary concerns, as well as ease of launching.

Until the appointment of Charles Cooke (1830–88) as the Institution's first Honorary Architect and Surveyor, the provision of premises in which to protect and maintain lifeboats had been a fairly ad hoc business. The standardization of lifeboats, as well as the greater availability of funds following a reorganization of the Institution, changed that. In the 30 years between his appointment and his death, nearly 300 boathouses were built to Cooke's design, as well as related slipways and breakwaters. His first commission, and the only lifeboat station he designed

RIGHT | Muskoka Boathouse, Canada (2001), designed by architects Brigitte Shim and Howard Sutcliffe. The boathouse straddles the boundary between Lake Muskoka and the thick mixed forest (see pages 132–137).

outside the British Isles and Ireland, was for a facility in Colombo, Ceylon (Sri Lanka). It was described in the *Civil Engineer and Architect's Journal*, in August 1858:

It has been mainly designed to keep the boats as much as possible from being injured by the heat. For this purpose there are two walls, the inside one being of cabook, a native stone, with a hollow space of one foot between the interior and exterior walls, which are of brick, with stone dressings, and strong bond-stores through both walls; the building is arched over in a similar manner. The roof, which is covered with tiles, projects considerably over the sides, and beneath it, between the buttresses are placed seats.

In general form and plan, the Colombo boathouse established Cooke's template. His boathouses for the Institute were typically built of local stone with a pitched roof (tiled) and overhanging eaves providing protection from the elements along the side walls. They were typically 40ft (12.2m) long and 17ft (5.2m) wide, with doors 14ft (4.3m) wide and 12ft (3.7m) high.

These rugged little buildings were designed primarily for practicality (see Walmer, pages 72–75). But while the scale and form of the lifeboat stations did not vary enormously, the finishes, detailing and general extent of architectural flourishes certainly did. The difference was determined by the wealth of the benefactor(s) behind them. The lifeboat house at Clacton-on-Sea (built 1878), on England's east coast, is a case in point. The elaborate High Victorian building, complete with octagonal tower, was built of red brick with a slate roof in a prominent location in the then fashionable Essex 'watering place'. On 15 September 1983 the *Builder* recorded that, 'the expense was met from the munificent gift voted to the institution by the Freemasons of England in testimony to their loyal gratitude on the occasion of the safe return of their Grand Master, HRH the Prince of Wales, from his tour through India.' The building remains in use as a pub: The Old Lifeboat House.

The size of the lifeboat and the ease of launching have traditionally determined the form, appearance and location of lifeboat houses. Until the introduction of motor-powered launches, in the early twentieth century, nearly all lifeboats were borne on carriages that were drawn to the water's edge by horses, at which point the carriage was turned around, the crew took their places in the boat, and the ground crew propelled the carriage into the water. The process was time-consuming and required large numbers of volunteers. As time passed, boathouses with integrated slipways built as close as possible to the waterfront became the most common model, dispensing with the need for large crews. Today, lifeboats are typically launched from slipways (see Clovelly, pages 82–83 and Tenby, pages 148–151), although davit-hung boat launches, where the lifeboat is carried on ropes over the water, perhaps from a pier or jetty, are another alternative.

Today

The diversity of contemporary boathouses is almost limitless. Examples in the last chapter (see pages 118–171) include a transparent arch carried on a frame of compressed paper tubes and a two-storey house with integrated wet dock floating on the water's surface. But while there are few technical boundaries, many countries impose strict restrictions on the construction of new boathouses in an effort to mitigate their environmental impacts.

Construction near the water's edge, or over the water, has the potential to cause erosion, disturb vulnerable shoreline habitats and fish breeding grounds and compromise the aesthetic appearance of sites of great natural beauty.

Human habitation of boathouses is also prohibited in many areas, in order to minimise impacts, and the amount of effluent. In some parts of the world there is also a growing interest in maintaining public access to waterfront sites by keeping private ownership to a minimum.

Taken in composite, these restrictions may appear to imply the end of an era in boathouse construction. The truth is probably less dramatic. The potential for construction on new sites may be increasingly limited, but as we have seen, the tradition of recycling sites is an ingrained aspect of this ancient building type.

EIGHTEENTH-CENTURY BOATHOUSES

BOTNY DOMIK

PETER-PAUL FORTRESS, ST PETERSBURG, RUSSIA (1765)

Botny domik (little boathouse) is a mausoleum. It was built to house the *Botik* (little boat), the vessel on which Peter the Great, founder of the Russian Navy, learned to sail.

The *Botik* was built in England during the 1640s. It originally belonged to Peter's grandfather, the boyar Nikita Ivanovich Romanov. Legend has it that the young Peter discovered the boat in the 1680s, had it restored and over the following years mastered the art of sailing on the waterways around Moscow. The experience inspired his study of boat design and construction in Amsterdam, Saardam and London, and later the emergence of a Russian naval fleet.

Between 1704 and the Treaty of Nystad in 1721, a series of naval successes under Peter's command saw ultimate Russian victory in the Great Northern War. During this period the *Botik* was stored at the Kremlin in Moscow. In 1722 it was transported to St Petersburg, the new 'northern capital' founded by Peter in 1703. During military parades held to commemorate Russia's emergence as a major military power the *Botik* was celebrated as the 'Grandfather of the Russian Fleet'. Two years later Peter the Great died, and the *Botik* was relocated to the Kronverk at the Peter-Paul Fortress. Botny domik, standing in front of the Peter and Paul Cathedral where Peter is buried, was built as its permanent resting place.

Construction of the baroque stone pavilion began in 1762, to designs by architect Alexander Vist. A classical portico leads to the essentially square main body of the structure, which incorporates a central hall flanked by two wings. The mansard roof is surmounted by a podium and statue of a classically posed woman holding a paddle, a symbol of navigation. The original wooden statue has been replaced twice. The present terracotta replica dates to 1891.

In 1928, during the Communist era, the *Botik* was relocated to Peterhof, the country estate of Peter the Great, near St Petersburg. Since 1940 it has been housed in the Central Naval Museum, in St Petersburg. A replica was built for display in the Botny domik.

FAR LEFT | Botny domik is located in front of the cathedral (1733) at the Peter-Paul Fortress, where Peter the Great established Russia's 'northern capital' in 1703.

BELOW | The baroque boathouse was built as a mausoleum to house the *Botik*, the small timber vessel revered as the 'Grandfather of the Russian Fleet'.

TRADITIONAL SOUTH SEA BOATHOUSES

SOCIETY ISLANDS (FRENCH POLYNESIA), SOUTH PACIFIC (RECORDED 1769)

LEFT | Scene from the
Society Islands,
including a traditional
boathouse and canoes.
Engraved from sketches
by Sydney Parkinson.

First Lieutenant James Cook sailed from Plymouth in late August 1768. Cook's patron, the Royal Society, had given him two challenges. The first was to chart the Transit of Venus in Tahiti on 3 June 1769. The second was sealed in an envelope, not to be opened until the first task was complete.

His Majesty's Bark *Endeavour* reached Tahiti in April 1769. Cook spent the weeks leading up to the Transit trying to establish cordial relations with the islanders, and setting up his portable observatory. The reason for charting the Transit of Venus was to establish the distance of the earth from the sun. The results were inconclusive, a consequence of the edges of Venus appearing blurred through the telescope.

Before leaving the Society Islands, Cook and the crew of the *Endeavour* spent a month exploring the neighbouring islands and atolls to the northwest; Cook named the archipelago the Society Islands, in honour of his patron. As they did throughout the three-year voyage, Cook, botanist Joseph Banks and ship's artist Sydney Parkinson described and illustrated their observations. The seafaring skills, carved canoes and elaborate boathouses of the Melanesians featured prominently in their records.

The first island visited by the *Endeavour* was Huahine (Huaheine). Banks's diary records: 'We went on shore ... and walked up the hills, where the productions were exactly the same as those of Otaheite [Tahiti] .... The houses were neat, and the boathouses were remarkably large; one that we measured was fifty paces long, ten broad, and twenty-four feet high; the whole formed a pointed arch, like those of our old cathedrals, which was supported on one side by twenty-six, and on the other side by thirty pillars, or rather posts, about two feet high, and one thick, upon most of which were rudely carved the heads of men, and several fanciful devices, not altogether unlike those which we sometimes see printed from wooden blocks, at the beginning and end of old books.'

Another diary entry, perhaps attributable to Parkinson, states: 'There is a great number of boat-houses all round the bays, built with a Catanarian arch, thatched all over; and the boats kept in them are very long, bellying out on the sides, with a very high peaked stern, and are used only at particular seasons.'

By 20 July the *Endeavour* had reached Raiatea (referred to by the diarists as Ulietea and Yoolee-Etea), the second largest island in the Polynesian archipelago. The following day Banks recorded: 'Dr Solander and myself walkd out this morn and saw many large Boathouses like that describd at Huahine. On these the inhabitants were at work making and repairing the large Canoes calld by them *Pahee*, at which business they workd with incredible cleverness tho their tools certainly were as bad as possible ...'.

During their stay on Raiatea, Parkinson drew several pictures of the boathouses. The most detailed, which may be a composite of illustrations prepared for publication, shows a large double canoe with a ten-strong crew – as well as a pig and at least one chicken – harvesting fish. In the foreground a group of Melanesians assess their catch. A large boathouse to the left of the image houses a double canoe. It is composed of a lightweight timber frame enclosed with vegetable matter. There are a further two long boathouses in the background.

Other sketches and illustrations show a canoe house built on piles standing in the water, and another shows a variety of barrel-vaulted structures made of local materials.

With the tour of the Society Islands complete, Cook turned his attention to the second instruction: to travel south in search of the great Southern Continent, believed to exist as a counter-weight to the northern lands, to chart New Zealand and to claim any unknown lands that he came across in the name of King George III.

ABOVE | Sydney Parkinson's illustration showing, 'A Boat-House, in which the Natives of Yoolee-Etea, and the Neighbouring Islands, preserve their Canoes of State from the Weather', 1769.

FISHING ROOM AND BOATHOUSE

KEDLESTON HALL, DERBYSHIRE, ENGLAND (1772)

In December 1758, Scottish classical architect Robert Adam wrote to his brother James in Rome. The letter described his joy at a recent appointment. He had 'got the intire [sic] management of his [Sir Nathaniel Curzon's] Grounds put into my hands with full powers as to Temples Bridges Seats & Cascades.... A noble piece of water, a man resolved to spare no Expense.'

Fourteen years later the Fishing Room and Boathouse, arguably the most elaborate and picturesque of the many structures that Adam designed for Sir Nathaniel (later Lord Scarsdale) in the grounds of Kedleston Hall, was complete.

The 'naturalization' of Kedleston's formal gardens had begun prior to Adam's appointment. Based on a plan devised by landscape gardener William Emes, the existing formal canals connected by a series of weirs was broken up into a sequence of irregularly shaped and independent lakes. One consequence of these changes was that if the Upper Lake, the water body closest to the entrance to the grounds, was to have any recreational use it would need a boathouse of its own.

The combined Fishing Room and Boathouse – it also includes a cold bath – was among the first buildings that Adam designed for Kedleston. It was an opportunity for Sir Nathaniel to impress guests upon arrival, and for Adam to fine-tune his 'antique' style.

The building is composed of three bays: two single-storey boathouses either side of a double height central section that houses the fishing room above the cold bath. The building is entered from the park side through a modest façade with a recessed porch flanked by two simple windows. Above the windows are roundels carved with putti riding sea horses The protruding roofs of the boathouses were originally masked by weeping willows.

LEFT | The building's modest park-side façade belies the elegance of its interior.

BELOW | The small classical building comprises two boat docks either side of a central bay, with a cold bath below and fishing room above.

BELOW, BELOW RIGHT AND BOTTOM | The interior of the Fishing Room.

RIGHT | Wet docks flank the central cold bath on the ground floor.

Inside is a small, richly decorated room dominated by an Ionic Venetian window opposite the entrance, a chimneypiece on one wall and a tall rectangular recess on the other. A fountain of entwined dolphins was intended for the recess, but it is not thought to have been executed. All the ornamentation is appropriately maritime, including a wave motif on the dado, and stylized scallop shells on the frieze and architrave.

It is not clear how much fishing happened in the Fishing Room. Its limited dimensions (12x15ft/3.6x4m) and sash window would have been significant impediments to the serious fisherman. It may have seen greater use as a comfortable place for a boating party, or to warm up in front of the fire after a cold bath.

Kedleston's natural spring of cold sulphurous water was highly thought of in the eighteenth century. At one stage Sir Nathaniel considered establishing a medicinal spa on the estate. The water for the small semicircular cold bath was originally channelled from Bentley Well about half way between the Fishing Room and the main house.

The Fishing Room is one of only a handful built in Britain. Others were at Beckett in Berkshire (c.1635) and Enville Hall in Staffordshire (1769). There is also Izaak Walton's relatively modest Fishing Temple up the River Dove from Kedleston in Beresford Dale (1674).

NINETEENTH-CENTURY BOATHOUSES

OBERSEE BOATHOUSE

BERCHTESGADEN NATIONAL PARK, BAVARIA, GERMANY (EARLY-1800s)

The Berchtesgaden Alps straddle the border between Germany and Austria. It is a serene glacial landscape characterized by steep alpine peaks with deep lakes in the valleys in between.

It is believed that there has been a boathouse on the east shore of Obersee (Upper Lake) for over 500 years. The present building is comparatively recent, although some structural elements, including the piles and perhaps some of the vertical timber cladding and roofing boards, date to the early 1800s, when a sluice was created in the moraine embankment that separates Obersee from Königssee (King's Lake) to the north. The sluice opened up a trade route for loggers farming the banks of Obersee and transporting their spoils through Königssee to Berchtesgaden.

Loggers built the low, pitched roof boathouse in the shallows, using it as shelter for their vulnerable two-seated vessels, of which there are believed to have been only a handful on the lakes at the peak of the trade. The shallow-draught 'Laner' boats entered through an opening at the lakeside end of the boathouse. A smaller doorway opens to a causeway, now submerged, that links the boathouse to the gravel shore.

RIGHT | The Obersee boathouse was built by loggers and used as a shelter for their shallow-draught vessels.

GREENWAY BOATHOUSE

GREENWAY, DEVON, ENGLAND (1820s)

They passed the folly and zigzagged down the path to the river. The outlines of the boathouse showed beneath them. Poirot remarked that it would be awkward if the murder searchers were to light upon the boathouse and find the body by accident.

A short steep slope led down to the door of the boathouse, which was built out over the river, with a little wharf and a storage place for boats underneath

'We've just come to cheer you up, Marlene,' [Mrs Oliver] said brightly as she entered. Marlene made no response. She lay quite motionless.

Poirot was frowning. Very gently he pushed Mrs Oliver aside and went and bent over the girl on the floor. A suppressed exclamation came from his lips. He looked up to Mrs Oliver. 'So ...' he said. 'That which you expected has happened.'

'You don't mean ...' Mrs Oliver's eyes widened in horror. She grasped one of the basket chairs and sat down. 'You don't mean ... She isn't dead?' Poirot nodded.

Passage from *Dead Man's Folly* by Agatha Christie

X

FAR LEFT | The two-storey former bathing house and single-storey stone boathouse both occupy Greenway Quay.

LEFT | The balcony and upper elevation are clad in timber shingles.

The two-storey boathouse at Greenway was the setting for the murder of teenage Girl Guide Marlene Tucker in Agatha Christie's 1956 novel *Dead Man's Folly*, in which Belgian sleuth Hercule Poirot is engaged to investigate suspicious goings-on during preparations for a weekend Murder Hunt, a variation on a Treasure Hunt, organized by detective novelist Ariadne Oliver.

Between 1938 and 1959, Greenway ('Nasse' in *Dead Man's Folly*) was the summer home of Christie and her husband, archeologist Max Mallowan. The picturesque estate is perched on a hill spur projecting into the River Dart, north of Torquay, the Devon seaside resort where Christie was born and brought up. The upper level of the boathouse, a sparsely furnished 'summer room' with a fireplace and balcony overlooking the Dart, was one of her favourite places for writing.

Greenway was first recorded in 1493 as 'Greynway', a crossing point of the Dart to Dittisham. A Tudor mansion was built in the late sixteenth century, possibly on the site of the present house, an elegant Georgian mansion built in the 1790s by Edward Elton, a merchant, adventurer and Member of Parliament. It is thought that his son James Marwood Elton commissioned the two-storey boathouse sometime in the early nineteenth century. Elton junior also oversaw a redevelopment of the grounds in the style of Humphry Repton. The 30-acre estate, with abundant exotic plants and trees, retains much of its Reptonian character.

There are actually two boathouses at 'Greenway Quay', the two-storey building with projecting balcony, and an adjacent single-storey structure built at a later date. As originally built, the lower storey of the original boathouse may have been used as a bathing house, fed by the tide of the Dart. Today, this lower level, with three modified window openings facing the river, is a changing room and storage space. The single-storey stone boathouse, which has a dedicated slipway, is still used for boat storage.

THE DYLAN THOMAS BOATHOUSE

LAUGHARNE, CARMARTHENSHIRE, WALES (1800–1850s)

FAR LEFT AND LEFT |
The Dylan Thomas
Boathouse stands hard
on a sandstone cliff
facing the shallow
estuary of Afon Taff.

The Dylan Thomas Boathouse is not actually a boathouse. As originally built, sometime in the early nineteenth century, an opening in the wall to the left of the house, as viewed from the estuary, led to a boat enclosure, but it was blocked up long ago. Today, the name is a rare remnant of the origins of the pretty two-bedroom, slate-roofed cottage.

For generations the boathouse was home to the ferry-men who offered transport across the estuary to Llansteffan. In the 1920s, it was owned by a Dr Cowan, who built a shed for his Wolsey at the top of the cliff about 100 yards above the boathouse. In 1949, Welsh actress and Dylan Thomas patron-ess, Margaret Taylor, bought the boathouse and loaned it to the debt-burdened family. Thomas, his wife Caitlin, their two children – soon to be three – and a dog took up residence in May of that year.

The boathouse, which is at the bottom of a sandstone cliff behind the ruins of Laugharne Castle, was home to Dylan Thomas (1914–1953) for the last four years of his often tempestuous life.

Some of his most renowned works, including *Under Milk Wood*, were written in Dr Cowan's old car shed, which Thomas convert-ed to his study and retreat, and which he memorably described as a, 'sea-shaken house on the breakneck of rocks'.

Following Thomas's death during an American lecture tour, at the age of only 39, Caitlin and the children lived on at the boathouse until 1958. In the mid-1970s, and by then falling into decay, the house was sold to a Thomas Trust, and subse-quently to Carmarthenshire County Council, which still owns and manages the building. Today it houses the Dylan Thomas Heritage Centre.

When funds permit Carmarthenshire County Council plans to re-establish the boathouse in its original configuration, with an opening to the estuary.

The Dylan Thomas Heritage Centre is open throughout the year, www.dylanthomasboathouse.com

SCOTNEY CASTLE BOATHOUSE

SCOTNEY NEW CASTLE, KENT, ENGLAND (1840s)

The romantic, timber-framed boathouse at Scotney Castle was built during the early-Victorian period, when the estate took on its present character, with a large Tudor-style house set within a Picturesque Revival garden.

Scotney Old Castle dates to the late-1300s, when Roger Ashburnham built a fortified manor house, possibly in response to the threat of French invasion. In the early-1400s the estate passed into the hands of the Darell family, who oversaw the addition of an Elizabethan south wing in the 1580s, and a much grander east range, in the style of Inigo Jones, in the 1630s. It was in this state that Edward Hussey bought Scotney in 1778. His grandson, Edward Hussey III, was the man responsible for the contemporary version of Scotney.

Hussey III moved to Kent in 1835 and set about transforming the estate. By then the old castle was in a state of disrepair. Instead of investing in an expensive restoration, he commissioned architect Anthony Salvin (1799–1881), a noted medievalist, to design a new house on a terrace overlooking the lake.

Scotney New Castle is an example of the revival of interest in Tudor architecture during the early nineteenth century. Construction of the asymmetrical composition began in the late-1830s and was complete by 1843. The sandstone was quarried on the estate. The hole that it left behind was turned into a Quarry Garden, complete with a dinosaur footprint, said to be 100 million years old.

Prolific landscape gardener William Sawrey Gilpin (1762–1843) oversaw the design for the new Picturesque Revival garden in collaboration with Hussey III. Its centrepiece is the artfully decayed ruin of the Old Castle, a moated medieval manor house.

The boathouse, one of a number of subsidiary buildings within the garden, is a simple timber-framed structure clad in vertical timber boards, with carved bargeboards and red roof tiles. It is supported on piles standing in the water and is accessed via a path in the garden. During the summer it is concealed in abundant undergrowth.

LEFT | The romantic timber boathouse dates to the 1840s.

BELOW | Approached from the garden, the boathouse appears to have sunk into the landscape.

WRAY CASTLE BOATHOUSE

AMBLESIDE, CUMBRIA, ENGLAND (1840s)

Legend has it that Liverpool surgeon Dr James Dawson spent his wife's inherited gin fortune on Wray Castle, which was designed in the 1830s by architect H P Horner, who later drank himself to his grave. Mrs Dawson took one look at the Gothic Revival pile before refusing to move in. Undeterred, Dr Dawson lived there until 1875, when he died at the age of 96.

As well as the theatrical Gothic mansion house, complete with imposing turrets and mock fortifications, Dr Dawson oversaw the construction of a nearby church, for the 'spiritual benefit' of the community, and a bulky castellated boathouse on the northwest shore of Lake Windermere.

The boathouse is entered from Watbarrow Wood via a short flight of suitably baronial stairs. The two-storey structure, strangely staggered in plan, includes a viewing gallery looking over the lake, with wet docks below. Two pointed arch openings lead to the lake. The composition is shielded on both sides by stone embankments. Later additions include timber doors to the two lakeside openings, and a timber jetty accessed directly from the wood.

Wray Castle has impressive associations with Lake District literary lions. William Wordsworth planted a mulberry tree at the estate in 1845. A plaque commemorates the event. He later described the castle as adding, 'a dignified feature to the interesting scenery in the midst of which it stands'.

Beatrix Potter was also much taken with Wray. In 1882, when the budding writer was sixteen, the Potter family rented Wray for a summer holiday. During their stay, the young Beatrix was encouraged to write *The Tale of Peter Rabbit* by Canon H Rawnsley, the vicar of Wray Church and nephew of Dr Dawson. The visit was the start of her lifelong love affair with the Lakes.

In 1905 Potter bought nearby property Hill Top. As her success grew, she acquired a number of parcels of land surrounding Wray, but she never bought the castle itself which was passed to the National Trust in 1929.

It is sometimes possible to visit Wray Castle and the gardens, which include a fine range of specimen trees, are accessible to the public.

LEFT | Wray Castle and boathouse, 1886: the Gothic Revival estate was built in the 1840s.

RIGHT | The staggered two-storey stone boathouse is accessed from Watbarrow Wood.

HASLAR GUNBOAT YARD

GOSPORT, HAMPSHIRE, ENGLAND (1850s)

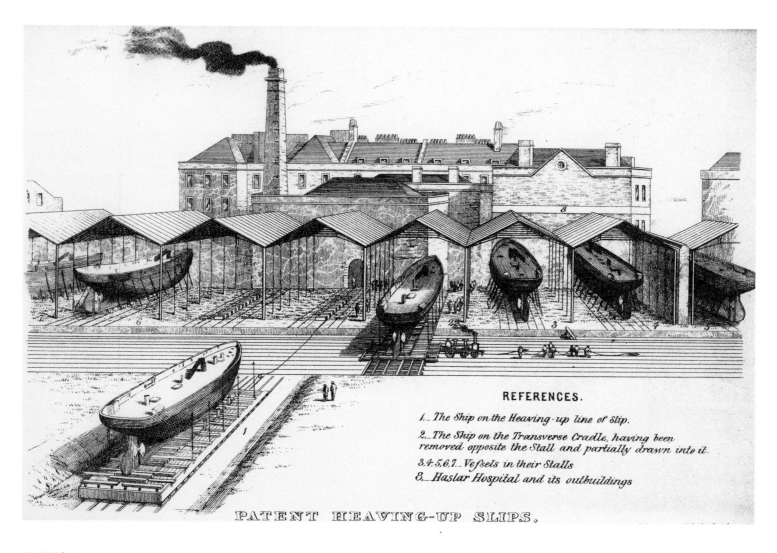

REFERENCES.

1._ The Ship on the Heaving-up line of Slip.

2._ The Ship on the Transverse Cradle, having been removed opposite the Stall and partially drawn into it.

3.4.5.6.7._ Vessels in their Stalls

8._ Haslar Hospital and its outbuildings

PATENT HEAVING-UP SLIPS.

ABOVE | The flotilla of light war craft built hastily after the Crimean War was stored under cover to allow the timber to season and to protect the iron from rust. *Mechanics' Magazine*, 3 January 1857

'Relations of Great Britain with foreign powers have been neither very close nor very cordial since the recent war [in the Crimea],' wrote the *Mechanics' Magazine* in January 1857. The bellicose atmosphere called for the construction of a 'vast and costly flotilla of light war craft', and time was of the essence.

From the middle of 1856, five classes of gunboats were constructed, some of timber, others of iron. The *Mechanics' Magazine* suspected that they were built 'with little regard to anything but the time named for their completion [as a consequence] unseasoned timber and careless workmanship must necessarily have been resorted to'. The editors regarded it as 'highly desirable that means should be provided for removing these vessels from the water, in order that planks might be taken out here and there, and other contrivances adopted for the double purpose of seasoning their timbers, and for necessary inspection and repairs'. The thinking behind taking the iron vessels from the water was that, 'they could be preserved from wear and rust better out of it than in it'. Existing facilities at Naval dockyards were designed for far larger vessels, and were in almost constant use. A new type of dry dock was called for.

Thomas White, a Portsmouth shipbuilder, came up with the solution. 'It occurred to Mr White that it would be convenient to stow the vessels in parallel tiers, side by side, and to place any number of them thus, by means of one principal slip-way, up which the whole might be successively drawn, and from which they might be removed on lateral rails to front their respective stalls.'

A tract of land adjacent to Haslar Hospital, in Gosport, was selected and prepared to receive 200 vessels. The first, the *Gnat*, was hauled up on 25 November 1856. The first ten vessels were stored under cover in separate pitched-roof bays carried on a series of cast iron columns and cast iron roof trusses. The whole was given rigidity by the walls of the hospital to the rear. It is not certain what material was used for the roof. Thick sheets of broad gauge corrugated iron, a material invented in 1829 but already well known to the Navy, is the most likely option.

Despite the anxiety, the following 20 years were relatively peaceful. During the 1860s and 1870s, British armed forces were primarily concerned with the suppression of colonial uprisings and trade conflicts in far-flung corners of the globe. Britain herself was rarely threatened. It was not until 1878 that the vast and costly fleet was readied for action, and once again the Russians were the foe.

On 4 May 1878 the *Illustrated London News* reported that, 'arrangements were being made to get ready for sea the flotilla of iron gun-boats which were built for service in the Baltic during the last Russian war but most of which have since that time been lying ingloriously on the slips at Haslar'. By then the rudimentary boat shelter had been extended and fitted with timber slat gable ends.

The Constantinople crisis had passed by the end of 1879. The flotilla continued to languish ingloriously. Today the Haslar Gunboat sheds survive, significantly modified and in poor condition, as part of the Haslar Marine Technology Park. The Yard was scheduled as an Ancient Monument in 1976.

SHEERNESS BOATHOUSE STORE

SHEERNESS, KENT, ENGLAND (1860)

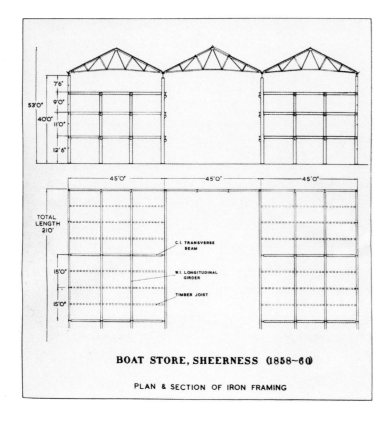

BOAT STORE, SHEERNESS (1858–60)

PLAN & SECTION OF IRON FRAMING

The Boat Store at Sheerness, completed in 1860, may be the world's oldest surviving multi-storey iron-framed building. In structural composition, detailing and quality it has been compared with the work of the mid-twentieth-century Modern masters, but it is unlikely that Walter Gropius, Mies van der Rohe or anyone else would have known anything about the Boat Store. It was designed by a little known military engineer for a secure military facility on an isolated stretch of the British coast near the mouth of the Thames. Its architectural significance lay unrecognized for almost a century after its completion.

In the summer of 1956, photographer Eric de Maré was commissioned by the Architectural Press to make a record of the best examples of England's early industrial architecture.

The search took him into a number of closely guarded naval dockyards. At Sheerness he came across the Boat Store: 'Its nautical trimness, and the long rhythmical, unadorned and dignified simplicity of its frame-and-fill construction made an immediate impact. It was impossible to date precisely from its general appearance, though it seemed to belong to the inter-war years,' wrote de Maré in 1961. Further research revealed that it was in fact designed in 1858, making it over a decade older than the Menier factory in France, until then believed to be the world's oldest multi-storeyed structure with an iron frame.

The Boat Store was designed by Colonel Godfrey Thomas Greene (1807–86), an engineer who served in India before 'retiring' to England in 1849, when he was appointed Director of Engineering and Architectural Works, Admiralty. The Boat Store was commissioned at a time of heightened military preparedness, following the protracted Crimean War (see also the previous entry) although it is unclear whether it was built for the storage of a particular class of vessel.

The following description of the building, by Professor A W Skempton, was published in the *Journal of the Royal Institute of British Architects* (volume 68) in 1961: 'The building consists of two identical buildings, or "aisles", either side of full-height void, or "nave". The whole is 210ft (64m) long and 135ft (41m) wide, with a skylight along the length of the roof over the nave, and windows extending from end to end of the two main external walls. The total height to the ridge is 53ft (16.2m). The nave is spanned by three travelling girders – one at each floor level – by means of which boats were hoisted up and manoeuvred into place on the upper floors.'

Today the Boat Store is heritage listed Grade 1.

RIGHT | Boats were hoisted to the upper levels by traveling girders spanning the central 'nave'.

BELOW | Sheerness Boat Store photographed in 1957, following its rediscovery by Eric de Maré.

VICTORIAN BOATHOUSE

TREVARNO, CORNWALL, ENGLAND (1870s)

FAR LEFT | Cloverleaf lead-light windows, ornamental bargeboards and a decorative turret distinguish the picturesque Victorian boathouse.

LEFT | The open-ended boathouse accommodates an embarkation platform and a small pleasure boat.

OVERLEAF | Extensive landscaping and plantings transformed the Trevarno Estate during the late nineteenth century.

To many of us, the challenge of boarding small boats is a searching test of dignity. The well-to-do women of British Victorian society, armed with parasols and wearing multi-layered summer dresses, would certainly not have relished the prospect, which may have been a driver behind the construction of this picturesque little boathouse and embarkation platform at the Trevarno Country Estate in Cornwall.

The boathouse was built in the mid-1870s, following the acquisition of Trevarno by the Bickford-Smith family. Their ancestor William Bickford had made the family fortune by inventing the Miners' Safety Fuse. The boathouse was one of many improvements to the estate during the late nineteenth century. The Bickford-Smiths were particularly active in shaping the landscape and grounds; over 30,000 trees were planted in 1883 alone.

The lake at Trevarno appears to have evolved from a pond, although there may have been a waterway of some type on the site for some time, as its lies on the path of a series of leats, which connected up with a series of water powered mines. The first edition Ordnance Survey map of 1877 indicates a water mass with a straight western flank, and the boathouse to the north.

The small timber-framed boathouse is carried on piles at the water's edge. It is entered from a path to the east. On the interior there is a hard-surfaced platform, running the length of the enclosure, and a rowing boat or punt. The structure is closed on three sides, and open to the lake at the south. Cloverleaf lead-light windows, ornamental bargeboards and a decorative turret surmounted by a weathervane distinguish the structure as an essentially intact relic of high Victoriana.

DUKE OF PORTLAND BOATHOUSE

ULLSWATER, CUMBRIA, LAKE DISTRICT, ENGLAND (c.1880s)

There has been a boathouse on this location, at the northern end of Ullswater, for over 200 years, probably longer. The aristocratic title of the present structure derives from the ownership of the site by William Bentinck, 3rd Duke of Portland (1738–1809) during the eighteenth century.

The Duke, who served at British Prime Minister in 1783 and 1807–09, owned extensive lands in Cumbria. He sold these assets, including the boathouse, in order to avoid bankruptcy following a protracted dispute over land rights in nearby Carlisle with Sir James Lowther, the 1st Earl of Lonsdale (1736–1802).

BELOW | Topography limits landside sightlines of the Duke of Portland Boathouse to one angle. Almost every picture of this Lake District landmark features the two-storey stone boathouse to the right of the frame, with a backdrop of undulating hills and reeds emerging from the lake in the foreground.

The present two-storey boathouse was built during the Victorian period, although its foundations are believed to date to the seventeenth century. The building comprises a slipway, jetty and enclosed wet dock, with a studio apartment above. The compact structure is made of stone, with a slate roof and a timber balcony projecting over the lake.

THE BOATHOUSES OF TIGRE

PARANÁ DELTA, ARGENTINA (1870s-MID 20TH CENTURY)

Tigre, a summer and weekend resort 30 kilometres north of Buenos Aires, has been described as 'Argentina's Henley'. Thirteen rowing clubs line the maze of waterways that surround the town, which occupies an island in the Paraná Delta, where the River Plate meets the River Paraná.

Many of the clubs were founded by the various immigrant groups that had a presence in the Argentine Republic during the country's late-nineteenth-century economic boom. They include the Buenos Aires Rowing Club, founded by British rowers, Club de Remo Teutonia (German), the Club de Regatas L'Aviron (French), Club Suizo de Buenos Aires (Swiss), Club de Regatas Hispano Argentino (Spanish), the Club de Remeros Escandinavos (Scandinavian), Club Canottieri Italiani and a Jewish club, Nautico Hacoaj. The boathouses are built in a myriad of architectural styles reflecting a confidence borne of prosperity and the liberation of the expatriate.

The first rowing regatta at Tigre was held on 10 December 1873. Six days later some of the British competitors, including the British minister in Buenos Aires, Lionel Sackville-West, founded the Buenos Aires Rowing Club. The club's boathouse and related facilities, including a restaurant, accommodation and tennis courts, were complete by the end of the 1870s. In its proportions and eclectic style the building set the template for Tigre's boathouses; the dominant elements of the principal building are a square four-storey tower with medieval slit windows and a pyramidal roof, and the curvaceous Dutch-style gable end of the main entrance.

The grandest of the Tigre boathouses is the Club de Regatas La Marina, a symmetrical four-storey Beaux Arts edifice on the River Paraná. In the centre of the roof is a circular belvedere, reminiscent of a Victorian bandstand; Tudor-style half-timbering defines the two upper levels. Access to the ground boat stores is via seven arches, with a stretched opening in the centre.

Other highlights of the Tigre boathouses include the Club Remo Argentino, which recalls the Club de Regatas La Marina in its application of terracotta tiles, half-timbering and broad ground floor arches; the Club de Regatas América, which appears to have been inspired by the colours and forms of a Mexican hacienda; and the Club Canottieri Italiani, a particularly distinguished building with decorative brickwork and a square tower. The Club Canottieri Italiani was once renowned for having the best Italian restaurant on the river.

RIGHT | The picturesque Club de Regatas La Marina is the grandest of the thirteen boathouses that line Tigre's waterways.

RIGHT | The Club Remo Argentino, with terracotta tiles, half-timbering and broad Edwardian arches.

BELOW | Curvaceous elevations and a flamboyant colour scheme suggest a Mexican influence in the Club de Regatas América.

LEFT | The Club Canottieri Italiani.

BELOW | Dating to the 1870s, the Buenos Aires Rowing Club is the oldest in Tigre. It was founded by British rowers, including Lionel Sackville-West, the British minister in Buenos Aires.

BOATHOUSE ROW

The ten boathouses that line the east bank of the Schuylkill River at Fairmount Park date from the 1870s. Each houses a separate rowing club, all of which are members of the 'Schuylkill Navy', the organization that oversees the management of rowing on the river.

The Fairmount Park stretch of the Schuylkill has long been associated with recreation. From the early days of settlement, in the late eighteenth century, Philadelphians swam and fished there. That recreational role intensified following the completion of the Fairmount Water Works and Dam in 1822, which transformed the Schuylkill from a tidal stream to a long freshwater lake whose placid surface was ideal for skating when frozen, and for rowing during the warmer months.

The first recorded rowing regatta on the Schuylkill took place in 1835, between the 'Blue Devils' and the 'Imps Barge Club'.

Its success led to the formation of several rowing clubs, the majority of them short-lived. As time passed the clubs that survived began to build premises, most of them ramshackle, utilitarian affairs.

In 1855 the City of Philadelphia – having purchased the area then known as the Lemon Hill Estate in 1844 – declared the area a public park. In 1859 all of the existing boathouses were condemned. Shortly after that the Park Commission was granted the authority to review and approve plans for new structures within the park. The first of the new generation of boathouses was completed in 1872. The bulky stone building, in the Victorian Gothic style favoured by the park architects, was followed by Picturesque Victorian, 'Shingle' and Colonial Revival-style boathouses. Materials other than stone were also permitted, including timber and stucco.

The present generation is no less diverse, including the steeply pitched roof of the Vesper Boat Club, painted a jaunty shade of red (no.10 Kelly Drive); the Gothic turrets of the Malta Boat Club (no.9); the mock-Tudor University Boat Club (nos. 7 and 8); the Prairie Style of the Crescent Boat Club (no.5); and the elegant Beaux-Arts-inspired Undine Barge Club (no.13), designed by eminent Philadelphia architect Frank Furness. (Furness also designed the Ringstetten boathouse, upriver, in 1876.)

By the 1960s, the boathouses were showing signs of dereliction, a state that jeapordized their continued existence in such a prominent and desirable riverfront location. From the middle of the decade vocal development groups began to lobby for their demolition. Throughout the 1970s a battle was waged between the developers and the Schuylkill Navy, the parent organization to the rowing clubs. A turning point came in1979 when architect Raymond Grenald designed a lighting installation that framed the dimensions of the boathouses. The outcome, particularly picturesque when reflected off the river, had the desired effect of attracting media attention to the boathouses' plight and increasing their visibility at night. Today the lights are one of the defining features of Boathouse Row – in 2005 the houses were fitted with LED lights that change colour throughout the year.

Boathouse Row, a National Historic Landmark, was elevated to the National Register of Historic Places in 1987.

BELOW | LED lights to frame the dimensions of the boat clubs were fitted in the late-1970s.

WALMER LIFEBOAT STATION

WALMER, KENT, ENGLAND (1871)

Goodwin Sands, on Kent's east coast, is one of the great natural dangers to shipping in British waters. It is estimated that over 2,000 vessels have come to grief on the low-lying seabed over the centuries. The remnants of some are visible from the Deal–Walmer foreshore at low tide.

In the 1860s funds were raised for the provision of a new lifeboat station at Walmer, to hasten access to shipwreck survivors. It was one of approximately 300 lifeboat stations designed by Charles Cooke, Honorary Architect and Surveyor to the National Lifeboat Institution between 1858 and 1888 (see pages 27–30). Apart from the addition of an extension to the seaward end the station has survived largely unmodified since its inauguration by Lady Victoria Levenson Gower in 1871.

In its essential form and arrangement the Walmer boat-house is almost identical to the first boathouse that Cooke designed for the Lifeboat Institute, at Colombo, Ceylon (Sri Lanka), in 1858.

As originally built, the oblong structure was 48.4ft/14.75m long and 35ft/10.5m wide with timber doors 14ft/4.2m wide at its seaward end and a smaller timber-framed arched doorway facing the town. A small bell tower, to raise the alarm, further distinguished the town-facing elevation.

The station was built of local Kentish rag with Bath stone dressings and a pitched roof enclosed with slate tiles. Over-hanging eaves formed open-ended verandahs with built-in timber benches along the side walls. Aside from a small viewing platform, the interior was a single open-plan volume. Viewed from a distance, Walmer Lifeboat Station resembles a modest chapel, or an elaborate bus shelter.

LEFT | The town-facing elevation, with bell tower and open-ended verandahs, is largely unaltered since 1871.

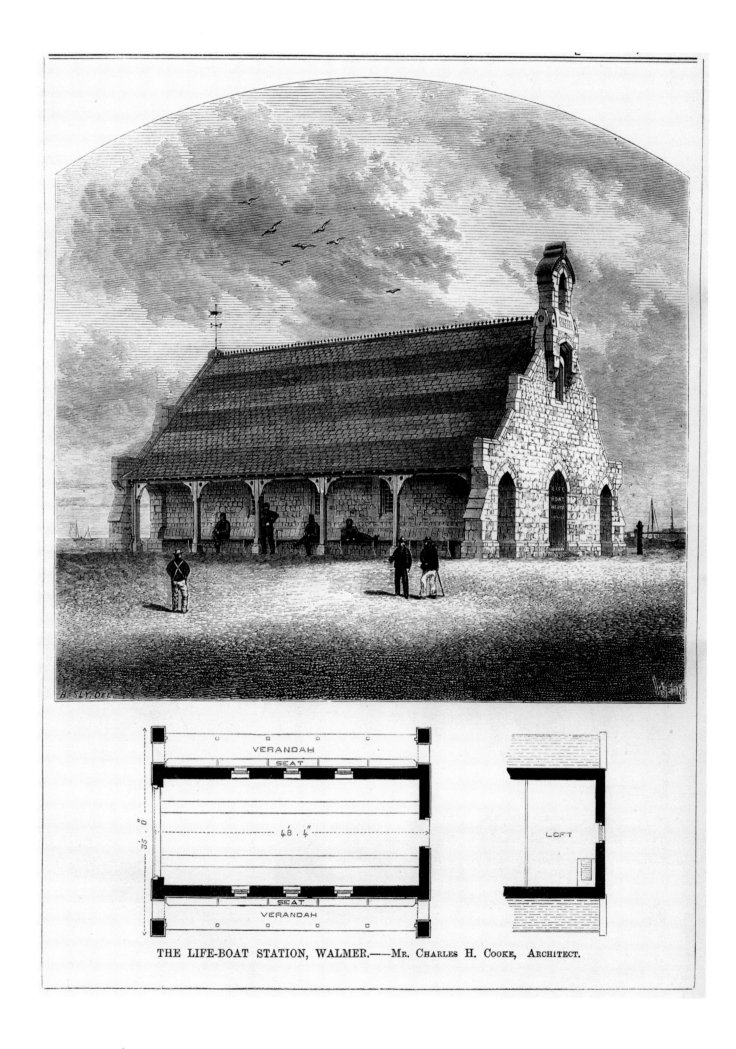

THE LIFE-BOAT STATION, WALMER.——Mr. Charles H. Cooke, Architect.

The building, erected by Messrs Denne of Deal at a total cost of £515, was well built and practical, and sufficiently flexible to adapt to changing technical requirements.

Until 1912, when the station was temporarily closed, it housed pulling and sailing lifeboats. It was equipped with a motor powered boat following its reopening in 1927. Proposals to upgrade the building in 1973, to accommodate a 37ft/11.2m boat were not carried out. Astonishingly, given the high turnover of lifeboat stations, this meant that it remained essentially untouched until 1991, when the seaward end was extended by 22ft/7m to accommodate the new Atlantic 21-type lifeboat and a launching tractor.

Today, with its premises nearing their 150th anniversary, Walmer is permanently established as an inshore lifeboat station. It accommodates an Atlantic 85 class lifeboat.

LEFT | Walmer Lifeboat Station was one of around 300 built to designs by Charles Cooke between 1858 and 1888.
ABOVE | The lifeboat station is in the heart of the small community. Walmer Lifeboat Station has been likened to a modest chapel, and an elaborate bus shelter.
RIGHT | The front door of the lifeboat station.

REALE SOCIETÀ CANOTTIERI CEREA

TURIN, ITALY (1886)

The Reale Società Canottieri Cerea is the oldest rowing club in Italy, dating to 1863. It was instrumental in the foundation of both the Federazione Italiana di Canottaggio (Italian Rowing Federation) in 1888, and the Féderation International du Sport d'Aviron (International Rowing Federation) in 1892. Over the years it has cultivated multiple Italian and World Champions, and Olympic medallists. Today, maintaining its male-only tradition, it has a 40-strong racing team. Cerea – a traditional greeting exchanged by boatmen crossing the River Po – also hosts one of the major events in the international rowing calendar, the Silver Skiff Regatta, a single scull race over a 7 mile (11km) course that draws more than 500 competitors each November.

Cerea's first base was a canvas shelter. Its current head-quarters, in the shadow of the grand Castello del Valentino on the north bank of the River Po, dates to 1886. The complex comprises two buildings: a clubhouse with overhanging pitched roof, and a double-fronted boat store with changing facilities above. There is a second boat store almost at water level, beneath the projecting terrace.

Due to the success of the Silver Skiff, and because of regular flooding to the lower boat store, plans are afoot for an extension to the southwest of the site. A timber-enclosed pavilion carried on pilotis has been designed by local architects MARC Studio (see pages 152–154), one of whose partners, Michele Bonino, is a former member of the Italian national rowing team. It will enclose a gym on the upper level, with the open-sided under-croft used for boat storage. Given the proximity of the building to the Castello del Valentino, a UNESCO World Heritage site in the centre of the north Italian city, there are a number of heritage procedures to go through before permission is granted for the works.

As well as Cerea's formative role in the foundations of professional rowing in Europe, the club is also associated with some heroic rowing feats. In 1868, a four rowed down the Po from Turin to Venice in five days; and in 1928 a coxed six circumnavigated the Italian peninsula and reached Rome rowing upstream along the River Tiber, a distance of 2,236 miles (3,600km) in 55 days.

Cerea was awarded its Reale (Royal) title in 1925.

FAR LEFT | Cerea is in the shadow of the seventeenth-century Castello del Valentino, a UNESCO World Heritage Site, on the north bank of the River Po.

ABOVE | The Reale Società Canottieri Cerea pictured towards the end of the nineteenth century.

BELOW | The Lodge Park boathouse is a rare
surviving corrugated iron kit building.

RIGHT | Corrugated iron manufacturer Francis Morton designed a shooting lodge with a concave roof profile for the 1862 International Exhibition.

BELOW | Boat House and Refreshment Room, with intersecting barrel vaults, designed by Francis Morton in 1873.

BELOW | Boathouse designed by Boulton and Paul, 1890s.

REGISTERED COPYRIGHT.

No. 329. PORTABLE IRON BOAT-HOUSE.

THE framework is of wood, covered with best galvanized corrugated iron. Outside woodwork painted three coats. Window glazed with 21-oz. sheet glass. Constructed in sections, ready for easy erection by purchaser.

Cash Prices, Carriage Paid.

12 ft. long; 6 ft. wide . £10 15 0

Prefabricated boathouses, hunting lodges and sports pavilions were just some of the buildings marketed at the 'country set' by manufacturers of corrugated iron buildings during the late-nineteenth century. These buildings were easy to erect – a useful attribute for seasonal buildings in isolated places – and sufficiently well appointed to satisfy the clientele's expectations.

The manufacturers were quick to respond to the trends of the day, which may explain the pagoda-style roof of the rare surviving boathouse at Lodge Park, on the Sherborne Estate in the Cotswolds. Japonisme was at the height of fashion in cultivated circles from the mid-1870s.

Lodge Park was built in 1634 by John 'Crump' Dutton, a *bon viveur* with a passion for gambling, banqueting and entertaining. The front elevation features a large viewing platform with views of the Cotswolds deer course and parkland. The house stayed in the Dutton family until 1983, when it was passed to the National Trust.

Little is known about the provenance of the boathouse, although Francis Morton, a major manufacturer of corrugated iron buildings based in Liverpool, is known to have designed buildings with a similar roof profile from the 1860s, such as the shooting lodge exhibited at the International Exhibition, London, 1862. The Lodge Park boathouse and side enclosure comprises a wet dock enclosed by sheets of corrugated iron carried on a cast iron frame.

The abundance of boathouses in manufacturers' catalogues reflects the contemporary popularity of boating, both for work and leisure. The options ranged from simple pitched-roof sheds erected over wet docks cut into river banks to much more elaborate affairs, such as the Boat House and Refreshment Rooms designed by Francis Morton in the 1870s, a strange concoction of intersecting barrel vaults. The larger wet dock supported the upper level refreshment room, with a balcony overlooking the water body. It is not known if the design was ever built.

CLOVELLY LIFEBOAT STATION

CLOVELLY, DEVON, ENGLAND (1893)

LEFT | Clovelly Lifeboat Station is located on Devon's exposed Bristol Channel coastline.

RIGHT | In the late 1990s the lifeboat station was extended to accommodate the new Atlantic 75 lifeboat and a launching tractor.

The lifeboat station at Clovelly is an unpretentious stone nugget plugging the gap between two weather-beaten terraces in the harbour of the North Devon fishing village. In scale, materials and composition it is perfectly suited to its setting.

The lifeboat station, with attached reinforced concrete slip, was built to improve launching into the harbour. It was located on the site of an earlier Royal National Lifeboat Institution facility, dating to the 1870s.

The replacement was completed to designs by W T Douglass, who became the second Honorary Architect to the Lifeboat Institution in 1888, following the death of Charles Cooke (see pages 29–30). Unlike his architect predecessor, Douglass was an engineer by training, perhaps reflecting the extent of technical expertise required of the job. During his tenure, Cooke received some recognition for designing around 300 lifeboat houses, but very little for the slipways and breakwaters so crucial to enabling lifeboats to launch in all weather. To reflect his successor's experience, and the nature of the challenge, his proper title was 'Engineer and Architect' to the Institution.

Douglass continued Cooke's use of heavy masonry construction and pitched roofs with overhanging eaves, but his style was generally more functional. Although modified since the 1890s, the Clovelly Lifeboat Station retains its essential character and form: a simple stone structure with a pitched roof enclosed by slate and top hung sliding doors opening to the sea. No doubt Douglass was constrained by the dimensions of the site and budget, as well as by considerations of practicality, the site being so close to the water's edge.

Between 1893 and 1988 the lifeboat station was in constant use by the RNLI. Following the end of that 95-year sequence it was operated independently by the Clovelly Trust, until 1998, when the RNLI took the station back within the fold. Soon after this, the building underwent an overhaul and expansion, to accommodate the new Atlantic 75 lifeboat, B-759 *Spirit of Clovelly*. The seaward end of the building was extended, in a style sympathetic with the original building, although the circular window in the seaward-facing gable is larger than the original.

TWENTIETH-CENTURY BOATHOUSES

RYOAN-JI BOATHOUSE

RYOAN-JI TEMPLE, KYOTO, JAPAN (DATE UNKNOWN)

The lake at Ryoan-ji (Temple of the Peaceful Dragon) was established in the twelfth century as part of an aristocrat's country estate. Today it is the wet counterpoint to one of Japan's most famous dry landscape gardens (*karesansui*), in which nature is compressed and given abstract expression within the confines of a narrow space.

The *karesansui*, a short distance north of Kyoyochi (Mandarin Duck Pond) is a small walled garden (82ft x 33ft/25m x 10m) in which fifteen stones are arranged in five groupings around raked white gravel. There is no vegetation, save for some moss around the stones. It is Zen landscape, intended to inspire philosophical meditation.

Throughout the past 800 years, a boathouse of some form has been perched on the shore of Kyoyochi, but almost nothing is recorded about these structures. In the exalted context of a revered *karesansui*, a humble, utilitarian boat shelter barely merits a mention. But it would have been there. Small boats were needed to reach the three islands and to allow visitors to appreciate the landscape and borrowed scenery from the centre of the lake, and shelters would have been required to protect the vessels from Japan's damp climate.

The form, scale and materials of the present boathouse, which appears to be a relatively recent structure, probably offer some accurate clues about its predecessors. The over-water

FAR LEFT | Boathouses have been a feature of the shore of Mandarin Duck Pond for around 800 years.

LEFT | Made of local materials, the boat shelter blends discreetly into the landscape.

BELOW | Steps cut into the shore of the lake lead down to the boat shelter.

shelter has an open-sided frame of rough-sawn timber and a shingle roof held in place with bamboo battens. Simple barge-boards to the lake-facing gable end add strength and a hint of refinement. A thick piece of bamboo, rising like a prow to the water, forms the ridgeline. Access is via a flight of steps formed in the north shore, leading to a small bamboo platform.

Like working boathouses around the world, the shelter at Ryoan-ji has been patched up and repaired as required. It is not flash or fancy, but it and its modest predecessors are as old as the landscape, and a fundamental component of what makes it work.

FRANK LLOYD WRIGHT'S FONTANA BOATHOUSE

BUFFALO, NEW YORK, USA (DESIGNED 1905; BUILT 2007)

LEFT AND RIGHT |
The boathouse is not
a complicated structure.
It embodied stylistic rather
than technical progress.

Frank Lloyd Wright (1867–1959) designed his 'Boathouse for the University of Wisconsin Boat Club' for a site in Madison, Wisconsin. Like many of the prolific architect's schemes, it was not built during his lifetime, but that did not stop him from regarding it as among his most significant works. The construction of the boathouse in 2007, nearly 50 years after Wright's death and more than a century after he originally conceptualised it, was the culmination of seven years of fund-raising and dedication by a not-for-profit organization called Frank Lloyd Wright's Rowing Boathouse Corporation.

Wright designed the University of Wisconsin Boat Club in 1905, without a firm commission. It came about at the request of Cudworth Beye, the commodore of the university's rowing crew and son of a family friend. The university had a fairly new boathouse (built 1892), located on Lake Mendota, but the water was choppy and froze in winter. Beye and his crew wanted a second boathouse on the banks of the Yahara River, a recently excavated channel between Lake Mendota and Lake Monona, where the water was comparatively warm and calm.

During the early years of the twentieth century, Wright was beginning to move away from his Prairie Style idiom, with brick-built structures characterized by minimal ornamentation and low-pitched or gable roofs, towards a greater level of abstraction. He was also beginning to experiment with materials, notably reinforced concrete. The Larkin Administration Building in Buffalo (1904) may be the earliest built evidence of this shift. The boathouse, which was incubated at around the same time, was a product of this mindset.

The ground floor comprised shelter for rowing shells, with docks for rowing shells to launch and land on either side. The upper level included a clubroom with lockers and baths. Writing to Beye in December 1905, Wright explained: 'The scheme is very simple, – tar and gravel roof, plastered walls and hemlock frame. The toilet arrangements are excessive and could be limited for the present to the arrangement at one end. Skylights light the aisles between the shells, so that they may be overhauled there; and provision has been made for a flue at either end, so that two stoves may be used if heat were necessary ...'.

BELOW | Drawings from the Wasmuth Portfolio, 1907.

BOTTOM | In 1931, Frank Lloyd Wright re-drew the boathouse for an exhibition that toured Holland, Belgium and Germany.

RIGHT | Side elevation: the boathouse was built largely as specified by Lloyd Wright.

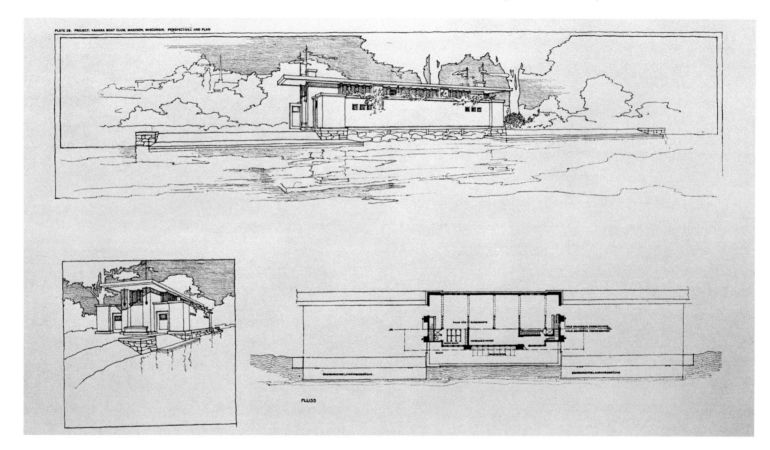

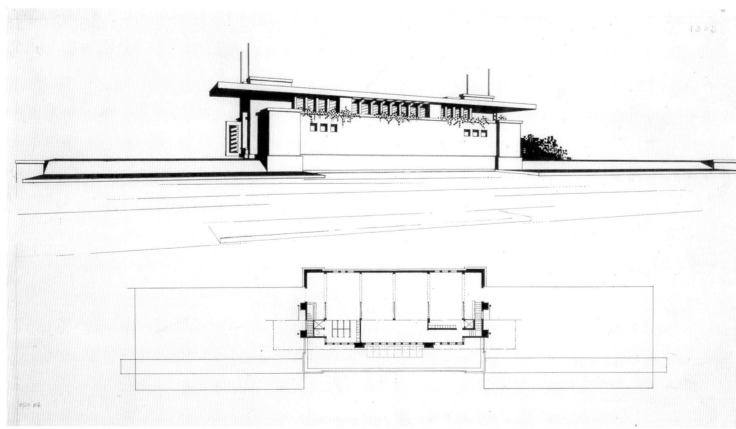

The building has long fascinated Wright aficionados and scholars. In 1942, American architectural historian, Henry-Russell Hitchcock, wrote: 'The little Yahara Boat Club was the first design in which Wright carried to its logical conclusions his interest in abstract composition .... Here in embryo we have the spirit of some of the most famous work of this decade and the next, the formal symmetry and emphasis on the cantilevered slab of Unity Church, 1906, and the dexterous and subtle elaboration of thickened planes and voids in space of the Coonley kindergarten project ...'. Hitchcock also emphasized, 'it is the boldly cantilevered slab roofs which give the Boat Club its particular significance'.

The University of Wisconsin decided not to back the project, and Cudworth Beye graduated soon afterwards, but to Wright, that was not the end of the boathouse. In 1907 he included it in an exhibition of drawings and models shown at the Art Institute of Chicago. Three years later it featured in the Wasmuth Portfolio (proper name, *Ausgefuehrte Bauten und Entwuerfe von Frank Lloyd Wright*), the architect's only monograph published in Berlin in 1910/11. Twenty years later it was still on his mind. A re-drawn version of the boathouse was one of eight schemes that Wright selected for an exhibition that toured Holland, Belgium and Germany in 1931. At that time he re-drew the boathouse as a concrete structure but changed little else. Wright regarded the exhibition as an opportunity to remind European modernists of the influence of his work on development of trends on that side of the Atlantic.

The story of how the boathouse finally came to be built dates to 1997 when John Courtin, then Executive Director of a not-for-profit corporation restoring Wright's Darwin D Martin House, saw the drawing at a Wright Scholars' Conference. Courtin, also a member of West Side Rowing Club, approached two other West Side members, Ted Marks and Jay Meyers and in 2000 they formed a corporation to build the boathouse in Buffalo. The logical site for the Wright boathouse was next to West Side Rowing Club, the largest youth-based rowing club in the USA. West Side was at capacity and needed the extra space the Wright designed boathouse would provide. In order to construct the boathouse as close to Wright's original vision as possible, the corporation worked with Anthony Puttnam, an architect from Madison Wisconsin and a former Wright apprentice. The building was completed in September 2007.

As envisaged in 1905, the boathouse includes two top-lit bays for racing shells on the ground level (80ft x 40ft/24m x 12m), and a clubroom with two locker rooms at the sides on the upper level (80ft x 20ft/24m x 6m). The rooftop viewing gallery can accommodate 165 people. The building has a concrete exterior, pine floors on the first floor and diamond-pane leaded glass just as Wright specified.

The boathouse is named after Charles and Marie Fontana. Charles was an oarsman and respected coach at West Side Rowing Club for several decades. His son, Tom Fontana is a successful TV writer and producer who made a $500,000 gift to the boathouse, which entitled him to naming rights. He named the boathouse in memory of his parents.

HUMBOLDT PARK BOATHOUSE

HUMBOLDT PARK, CHICAGO, USA (1907)

Respect for native landscapes and dedication to craftsmanship are among the principles that define the 'Prairie School', which evolved in the American Mid-West during the 1890s. Shallow hipped roofs, horizontal lines, overhanging eaves and discreet use of ornamentation are among its physical expressions. The Humboldt Park Boathouse is a rare surviving example of a Prairie-style building in a Prairie-style landscape.

Humboldt Park, named after Prussian naturalist, explorer and writer Alexander von Humboldt (1769–1859), was one of three pleasure gardens developed in Chicago's West Side during the 1870s. It is linked to Douglas and Garfield parks by a network of boulevards. They were a response to public concerns about the lack of parkland in the fast-growing city.

The man charged with developing plans for the West Side Parks was William Le Baron Jenney, who counted among his friends Frederick Law Olmsted, widely regarded as the father of American landscape architecture. Olmsted's naturalistic style was a significant influence on Jenney, as were the Parisian parks and boulevards, designed by Adolphe Alphand and Baron Haussmann, which Jenney had visited during the 1850s.

LEFT | The lake-facing
elevation pictured in 1908.

BELOW | Works to restore
the Humboldt Park
Boathouse began in 2002.

At Humboldt, Jenney was concerned with transforming the flat, swampy, broadly oblong site into a lush, picturesque landscape. His vision included winding paths to change views in the landscape and a large lake, a decorative feature that doubled as a drainage device. As originally envisaged, the main entrance led to a peninsula projecting into the lake. Jenney earmarked this as the site of a music pavilion.

Approximately 40 per cent of the 206-acre park, including part of the lake, had been developed according to Jenney's original vision by the time Humboldt Park was officially opened in 1877, the same year that Oscar F Dubuis superseded Jenney as the West Park Commission Engineer.

In the main, additions and alterations during Dubuis' tenure followed Jenney's naturalistic scheme. But the development of the park was sedate, caused initially by a lack of funds, and subsequently by corrupt management.

By 1905, when Danish immigrant Jens Jensen (1860–1951), was appointed to the West Park Commission as General Superintendent and Chief Landscape Architect, Humboldt Park had received little care or attention for a decade. It was in a poor state, a condition that gave Jensen the opportunity to experiment.

Since settling in Chicago in the mid-1880s, Jensen had been enchanted by Illinois' native landscape. He and his family made frequent trips to study plants in their natural environments. The improvements to Humboldt Park overseen by Jensen included a Prairie-style river, extending southwest from the lake, lined with reeds and other native marsh plants. He also introduced a rose garden, a formal arrangement of natural plants. The new buildings commissioned during this period were also in the Prairie style, which by the early twentieth century was associated principally with the offices of Louis Sullivan and Frank Lloyd Wright.

LEFT | The open-sided loggia mediated between the music court (left of picture, no longer extant) and the lake (right), pictured in 1908.

BELOW | A tree being transplanted during the winter of 1907/08.

One of the lesser-known architects working in the Prairie style was Hugh Mackie Gordon Garden, who had worked for both Sullivan and Lloyd Wright before going into partnership with Richard Schmidt in 1895; the partnership was later expanded to include structural engineer Edgar Martin. In 1906 Schmidt, Garden & Martin began work on the largest of a number of commissions that they undertook at Humboldt Park, the Music Court, close to the site of Jenney's proposed music pavilion. The formal rectangular open space was flanked to the south by a portable music shelter, and to the north by a boathouse. Both structures were characterized by a sense of openness and interaction with the landscape.

The music shelter – of which nothing remains – was a pergola-like composition with a portable bandstand. The two-storey pre-cast concrete boathouse mediated between the formal music court and the natural lakeside setting to its north.

The boathouse was built in 1907 to provide a landing point for rowers and a warm shelter for skaters during the winter. It sits on a single-storey base that was originally used for boat storage; the six doorways are no longer operable. The building's identical north and south façades are punctuated by three semicircular arches, and buttressed at either end by enclosed double-height pavilions, which included a refectory. The large central space on the upper level, with views to the north and south, still functions as an open-air viewing platform.

The Humboldt Park Boathouse is on the National Register of Historic Places and was designated a Chicago Landmark in 1996, by which time it had been largely unused for a decade and was in an advanced state of disrepair. A major restorative overhaul of the building, led by Chicago conservation architecture practice BauerLatoza Studio, began in 2002. In two phases, BauerLatoza oversaw the restoration of the building, and adaptive reuse of the interiors, to include an exhibition space, offices and a ticket hall.

QUEENSCLIFF LIFEBOAT STATION

QUEENSCLIFF, VICTORIA, AUSTRALIA (1929)

BELOW | Queenscliff lifeboat house was completed in 1929. The structure to the right was built in 1887, to accommodate passengers on the Bay Steamer run from Melbourne.

RIGHT | An enclosure (demolished) for a davit-hung lifeboat was built on the new Bay Steamer pier in the late-1880s.

The waters around Queenscliff, on the western flank of the entrance to Port Phillip Bay, are treacherous and unpredictable, caused by tidal flows surging between the narrow Bay entrance (the Rip) and Bass Strait to the south. There are shallow rock shelves on either side of deeper shipping channels. Early settlers were faced with the additional problem of rock pinnacles rising close to the water's surface (now removed). There are an estimated 20 wrecks in the immediate vicinity of the Port Phillip Heads, and at least 120 within a radius of ten nautical miles.

From the earliest years of settlement, in the mid-1830s, the vast majority of vessels servicing the growing British colony of the Port Phillip District (later Victoria) passed through the Rip en route to the metropolitan centres of Melbourne and Geelong. This made Queenscliff a site of great strategic significance: it was the perfect vantage point from which to monitor, direct and intercept shipping, and to reach vessels in distress.

The Port Phillip Pilots, watermen expert in negotiating through the Bay channels, offered the first lifesaving service, from the late-1830s. The first lifeboat was provided in 1856, at around the same time at the completion of the first pier at the town, known as Fisherman's Pier. A lifeboat shelter was built on the pier in 1860.

In the 1880s, Queenscliff Pier, stretching to deeper water, was constructed to provide a berth for the large 'Bay Steamers', then bringing hoards of tourists to the 'Victorian Ramsgate'. Towards the end of the 1880s, a hood-like enclosure was erected on the new pier to house a davit-hung lifeboat.

The present boathouse, a timber-framed structure with an integrated slipway, roller channel and keel-way was built between 1926 and 1929, for the *Queenscliffe*, a Watson Class boat built in Port Adelaide. In its barrel-shaped roof, cheap, lightweight materials (timber and corrugated metal sheeting) and in its positioning on stilts over water, it recalls the elevated slipway boathouse constructed in Britain from the early twentieth century (see pages 148–50, Tenby, 1904).

NOAH'S BOATHOUSE

BUCKINGHAMSHIRE, ENGLAND (1930)

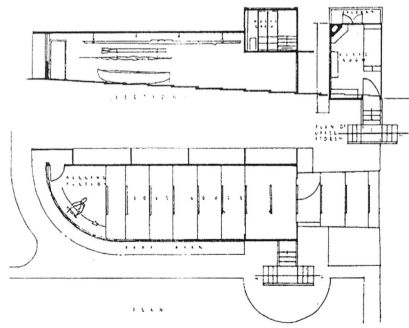

ABOVE | The boathouse and study formed part of an early experiment in Modern domestic architecture.

LEFT | Section and floor plans

RIGHT | Boat store: doors at the bottom of the raked concrete floor open to the River Thames.

FAR RIGHT | Detail of staircase to the study.

The boathouse at this Thames-side weekend retreat, built in the early-1930s, was part of an early experiment in Modern domestic architecture. The composition, materials and structure of the discrete complex of buildings were in marked contrast to the local vernacular, characterized by timber framing, exposed stonework and thatched roofs.

Architect Colin Lucas (1906–84) designed Noah's House and the related boathouse and outbuildings for his parents, Ralph Lucas, an inventor and entrepreneur, whose interests and lines of work included car design, construction and operating barges on the Thames, and Mary Anderson Juler, a composer, predominantly of orchestral and chamber works.

The family enjoyed weekends and summer holidays at a plot owned by Ralph on the Thames, near Bourne End. Accommodation was a houseboat, known as The Ark. When Colin graduated in architecture from Cambridge University in 1928, he joined forces with a builder and his father's construction business to create Lucas, Lloyd and Co., Architects and Builders. One of his first jobs was to design a permanent alternative to The Ark.

Cost was a concern, as was practicality; the site was only accessible by boat. So father and son decided to build the house of Thames ballast delivered to the site by barge. The ballast was used as an aggregate for all building elements, including the foundations, walls and roof.

The house, set back from the river's edge, was built in 1929. It was a composition of flat concrete planes, punctuated by voids and large expanses of glazing. The walls were originally painted terracotta brown. It was an impressive debut by an architect soon to join forces with Amyas Connell and Basil Ward to form one of Britain's leading Modern practices of the 1930s.

Construction of the boathouse began the following year. It comprised a workshop and boat store, for Ralph's nautical experiments, and a small study above, to give Mary solitude for composition. The lower level comprises a dry dock on a raked concrete floor opening onto a curved external workshop with the river below. Strip windows to the south and east elevations illuminate the boat store. The study is accessed from a staircase to the southeast.

As well as being a notable example of early Modern architecture, designed at a time of fierce opposition to such progressive ideas, Noah's House may be the first domestic building in Britain constructed entirely of reinforced concrete.

Sadly, the main house is much altered, although the concrete core of the building survives beneath the rendered walls and thatched roof. The boathouse – which is heritage listed – survives in a more authentic state, albeit in poor condition.

OXFORD BOATHOUSES

OXFORD, ENGLAND

Oxford does not want for boathouses. Punt stores, canoe clubs and boat builder's workshops line the banks of the Thames, or Isis, as the stretch of the Thames at Oxford is known locally. There are even a few of the old college barges around, a legacy of the early nineteenth century when Oxford University colleges used barges as clubrooms.

Beyond Christ Church Meadows and over a hump-backed bridge, a small triangular island at the intersection of the Isis with the River Cherwell is the epicentre of the college boathouses. The first of the ten boathouses that line the island's west bank was built by Christ Church in the mid-1930s. The river-facing elevation of the stripped classical edifice is composed of three bays, with the projecting central bay distinguished by a segmentally arched window on the upper level. An external staircase to the north provides access to the first floor clubrooms. Christ Church is a rare example of a mono-college boathouse; the majority are shared by two or three colleges. However, in its cheerless austerity, Christ Church did establish an architectural precedent for the college boathouses.

These are not lavish affairs. Wadham (shared with St Anne's and St Hugh's), at the upstream end of the island, is a simple cream brick building with metal roller doors to the boat stores. The Trinity and Merton college boathouses, further upstream, are the younger siblings of Christ Church, with stripped classical façades of red brick, albeit with pronounced stepped composi-tions and semi-castellated rooftop balustrades. The architectural highlight of the island boathouses, shared by Corpus Christi and St John's, is a conspicuously curvaceous confection with 1950s styling.

LEFT | View of the ten college boathouses on the small triangular island at the intersection of the Isis and River Cherwell, looking downstream.

The river-facing elevation comprises a ground floor boat store, projecting beyond the upper floor clubrooms, which is divided into two bays and finished in a pale render. Spiral staircases at either end provide access to the first floor clubrooms and a viewing terrace, which is formed by two elliptical concrete platforms. Straight flights of stairs lead to the rooftop viewing terrace. The dark floor-to-ceiling glazing of the clubrooms provides a stark contrast with the pale render of the ground level.

Until 1999, the opposite bank of the Isis was dominated by University College Boathouse, a substantial High Victorian structure built in the early-1880s. It also served as the base of the Oxford University Boat Club (OUB) and was the centre for rowing in Oxford. Its architect, John Oldrid Scott, the second son of Sir George Gilbert Scott, was known primarily for designing churches; the building was completed in 1882, the same year as the Greek Orthodox Cathedral in Bayswater, generally regarded as his masterpiece.

The three-storey structure built of face brick, comprised a river level boat store surmounted by clubrooms and a large viewing deck. It had a tiled roof of intersecting gables, with half-timbered gable ends. For over a century it was a well-known and well-used, if not universally admired, landmark on this stretch of the Isis. Sadly, in 1999 it was irreparably damaged in an arson attack. Its replacement, the premises of University College, adopts an altogether different architectural vocabulary, with a palette of materials including dark brick, stained cedar, reflective glazing and a flat copper roof inspired by the blade of an oar. It was designed by Belsize Architects, and completed in 2007.

FAR LEFT | Blue-painted timber doors and a segmentally arched window in the projecting central bay soften the austere stripped classicism of the Christ Church boathouse, the first in a row of ten college boathouses (1930s).

LEFT | The Corpus Christi and St John's boathouse is distinguished by curvaceous 1950s styling and contrasting materials, including pale render and dark-stained timber.

BELOW | University College Boathouse (2007), a replacement of the arson-damaged building of the 1880s.

CARMEL COLLEGE BOATHOUSES

WALLINGFORD, BERKSHIRE, ENGLAND (1890s & 1970)

FAR LEFT | Carmel College art gallery was a showcase of excellence in the arts and a memorial to Julius Gottlieb, an art lover and craftsman.

LEFT | The boathouse podium elevates the gallery in the landscape.

BELOW | Carmel College closed in 1970, but the Brutalist character of the boathouse endures.

A concrete pyramid surmounting a bunker-like red brick boathouse is one of the more unexpected features of the Thames near Oxford, indeed anywhere. It was designed as an addition to Carmel College, the 'Jewish Eton', in the late-1960s by Scottish architect Sir Basil Spence (1907–76) and it was in stark contrast to both the bucolic setting, and the existing boathouse on the estate.

Rabbi Kopul Rosen founded Carmel College in 1948. His vision was to establish an educational environment for Jewish children that combined the Lithuanian Yeshiva with aspects of the British public school system. The school was established in Newbury, moving in 1953 to Mongewell, a 70-acre estate outside Wallingford bordered to the west by a particularly straight stretch of the Thames.

The centrepiece of the estate was a three-storey Victorian pile that is rumoured to have been the inspiration for Monkswell Manor Guest House, in Agatha Christie's *Mousetrap*. This became the main school building. There was also a boathouse in the grounds, a two-storey half-timbered red brick structure with a flight of stairs on the side with access to the upper level.

Chaim Simons, a student at Carmel from 1953–60 recalls that rowing quickly became a popular pastime at the college and that within a few years the upper level became the meeting place of the Old Carmeli Association.

During the 1950s and 1960s, the college campus was expanded with classrooms, boarding houses and a dining room. In 1963 a wedge-shaped synagogue, fully glazed to three sides, was built to designs by local architect Thomas Hancock. The primacy of this progressive architectural gesture did not last long.

Carmel trustee Lieutenant Commander E J Gottlieb commissioned Spence to design the boathouse and art gallery as a showcase of excellence in the arts and a memorial to his late father Julius Gottlieb, an art lover and craftsman. To elevate the building in the landscape the pyramid was positioned on top of the rear of the low, single-storey boathouse composed of banked brick. The two boat openings face west, with a viewing deck above.

The pyramid, a form often associated with memorials, was originally intended to be a steel frame enclosed in zinc, but with costs spiralling concrete was used as a cheaper alternative. The gallery space is lit by pyramidal openings in the exterior walls. A sculpted bust of Julius Gottlieb is on permanent display.

The Carmel College boathouse and art gallery was officially opened by Lord Snowdon in June 1970.

The school closed in 1997, due to falling admissions and rising costs. Two years later the boathouse and gallery were listed Grade II*. The same year the nearby boathouse of University College, Oxford was razed in an arson attack. The Carmel boathouse became a temporary home for the club while the new building, completed in 2007, was under construction.

RIGHT | The old boathouse at Carmel College dates to the Victorian era.

MAORI *WAKA & KOROWAI*

WAITANGI TREATY GROUNDS, BAY OF ISLANDS, NEW ZEALAND (1975)

In the late 1930s one of the great Maori leaders, Princess Te Puea Herangi, commissioned the construction of a fleet of war canoes (*waka taua*) to commemorate the ancestor's journey to New Zealand (Aotearoa) from Polynesia. Her vision was to unite and uplift the Maori people ahead of the 1940 centennial of the Treaty of Waitangi, under which the European settlers and Maori people were intended to live together peaceably. Only three *waka* were complete in time for the 6 February anniversary. Her dream was fully realized in 1990 when 22 *waka* gathered at Waitangi for the 150th anniversary of the signing.

The centrepiece of the 1940 centennial was *Ngatoki-matawhaorua*, an 118 feet (36m) ceremonial war canoe built

LEFT | The carvings refer to Maori legends about the ancestors' voyages to New Zealand.

BELOW |
Ngatokimatawhaorua rests on timber supports on a base of sand.

with traditional techniques and materials. Two experts in *waka* construction were sent from Waikato to advise on the process. The Nga Puhi people supplied materials and labour. A kauri tree nine metres in circumference and three metres in diameter was selected for her mid section, a second provided the bow and stern. A team of bullocks moved the huge hull sections from the Puketi forest to Waipapa Landing, where they were soaked in a stream for three months. *Ngatokimatawhaorua* was completed by Christmas 1939.

On 7 February 1940 a meeting of the five northern Maori tribes, Nga Puhi, Te Rarawa, Aupouri, Ngati Kahu and Ngati Whatua, was held at Waitangi. The tribes decided to hand over

Ngatokimatawhaorua to the Waitangi National Trust Board for safekeeping. They asked that the meeting place (*marae*) be enlarged to accommodate a *waka* shelter, or *korowai*, to be built on the edge of Hobson's Bay. Architect William Page drew up the plans.

Ngatokimatawhaorua remained there until late-1973 when she was taken out and relaunched in preparation for the 1974 Waitangi Day celebrations which was renamed New Zealand Day that year. The present shelter was built in 1975. The structural frame is made of steel, and the roof is covered with wooden shakes (similar to shingles but larger and rougher).

The name *Ngatokimatawhaorua* is associated with two voyages from Polynesia to New Zealand. The first was by Kupe, who sailed around the North Island on his *waka*, *Matawhaorua*, before returning home to Hawaikii where he told his grandson Nuku-tawhiti of his sea route. Nukutawhiti enlarged *Matawhaorua* with two sacred adzes (*nga toki*) and renamed her *Ngatokimatawhaorua*. The carvings on the present *korowai* refer to these legends. On the ridge line, facing the sea is Nukutawhiti, grandson of Kupe. The bargeboards depict the octopus of Muturangi which Kupe chased into New Zealand waters.

FAR LEFT |
A carving of Nukutawhiti, grandson of Kupe, the ancestor who discovered the sea route around the North Island.

FAR LEFT BELOW | Oars are stored in the rafters.

LEFT | The original *waka* shelter, designed by architect William Page in the 1940s.

BELOW |
Ngatokimatawhaorua during the 1940 centennial of the Treaty of Waitangi.

'ARC' AT AALTO'S EXPERIMENTAL HOUSE

MUURATSALO, FINLAND (1998)

During the early 1950s, Finnish architect Alvar Aalto (1898–1976) built an experimental summerhouse on the island of Muuratsalo in central Finland. Aalto used the house as a test case for new materials and construction techniques. The column-free structure has no foundations. It also incorporates experiments with free-form brick construction and solar heating.

At the time Muuratsalo was an isolated wilderness. Roads on the island were unsealed tracks. The first bridge was not complete until 1948; Aalto designed a motorboat as the means of access. He named it *Nemo Propheta in Patria* (*Never a prophet in one's own country*), a reference to his sense of professional isolation at the time. The shallow draft, broad-beamed vessel was designed to land on the shallow beaches and headlands of Lake Päijänne. It had a short operational life, being cumbersome to manoeuvre and prone to leaking. It even sunk on a couple of occasions.

A few years after Aalto's death in 1976, *Nemo Propheta in Patria*, by then deemed unseaworthy, was transferred to the nearby town of Säynätsalo, where a protective shelter was built around it to the specifications of his widow Elissa.

Aalto's family continued to use the Experimental House until 1994, when Elissa handed it to the City of Jyväskylä. Today it is managed by the Alvar Aalto Museum, which runs guided tours of the property during the summer months.

In 1995, the museum, in collaboration with the City of Jyväskylä and Helsinki University of Technology, proposed to relocate *Nemo Propheta in Patria* to the Experimental House, and initiated a design competition for a shelter to protect it, on a site close to Aalto's original jetty.

RIGHT | 'Arc' is a mausoleum for a motorboat that was a component of Alvar Aalto's vision for his summerhouse. It is designed to blend with the woodland setting.

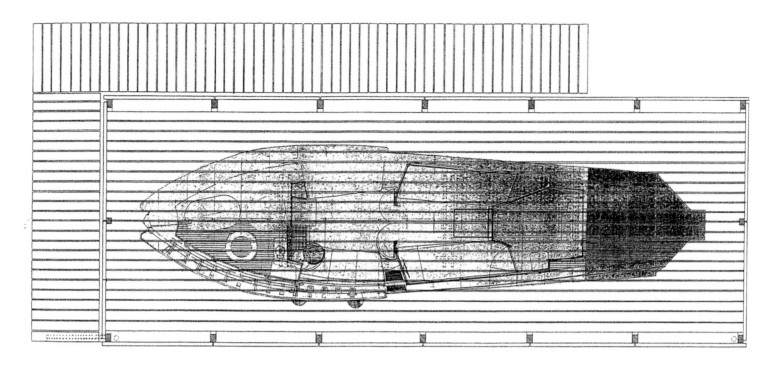

ABOVE AND BELOW |
Plan and section
for 'Arc'.

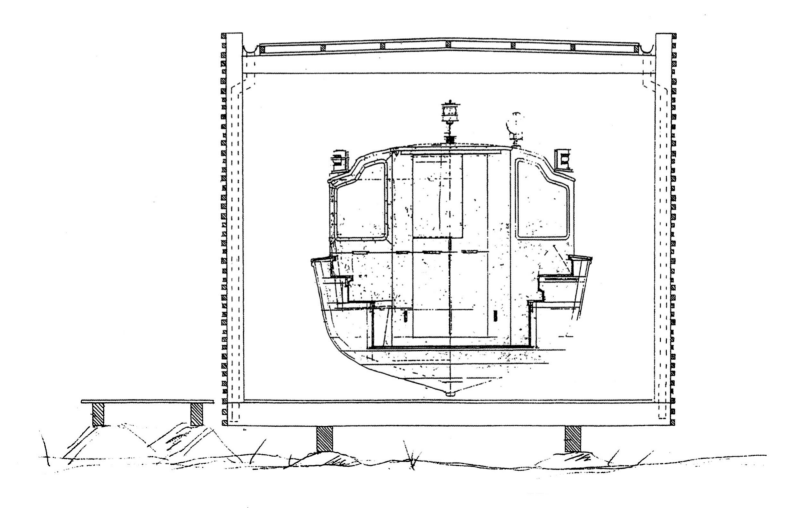

The ambition was to create a structure that allowed visitors to see the vessel from all angles, while simultaneously protecting it from animals and the harsh environment. 'Arc', the successful entry, designed by Danish architects Claudia Sculz and Anne-Mette Krolmark, is composed of strips of untreated larch attached horizontally to a pine frame, supported on a low-impact base nestled into the contours of the site.

The silhouette of the boat is visible through the open slats. The play of light with the lake behind mimics the flickering dance of sunlight in the woodland. During the winter the shelter is wrapped in a tarpaulin.

ABOVE | Alvar Aalto aboard *Nemo Propheta in Patria* in the 1950s. The building to the right is a traditional smoke sauna, designed by Aalto as part of his experimental summerhouse.

NORTHBRIDGE BOATSHED

SYDNEY, NEW SOUTH WALES, AUSTRALIA (1998)

An ambition to celebrate the romanticism of boathouses and optimize the beautiful setting on Sydney's Middle Harbour underpinned Jon King's approach to the design of the Northbridge Boathouse.

The small 23ft x 13ft/7m x 4m two-storey structure is located at the bottom of a steep 229ft/70m-long garden to a 1930s Art Deco house. The enduring appeal of the sunny, sheltered spot is evident in the variety of markings to the rock shelf adjacent to the boatshed, including fish symbols that may be aboriginal, and graffiti that apparently date to the nineteenth century.

The building accommodates a dry dock for small boats below, with a multi-purpose space with ribbon windows to all elevations above. Local hardwood panels, laid horizontally to the timber frame, and sandstone quarried on site express the different levels. The structure is enclosed with a copper roof, which has softened to a dark brown in the Australian climate.

The dry dock includes space for small boats and equipment. The upper level is equipped with a fridge and sink but is otherwise open planned. Top hung shutter-style windows to the north, east and south elevations can be opened to create the effect of an outdoor room. The space can seat 10–12 for dinner, and any number of sleeping bags for a summer sleepover.

The building, beautifully detailed in the style of a clinker boat, won the Royal Australian Institute for Architecture Boral Timber Award in 1998. After completion King received a number of enquiries for similar designs, none of which has come to fruition, a consequence of a crackdown by local authorities on construction abutting the water's edge. The Northbridge Boatshed was completed just in time.

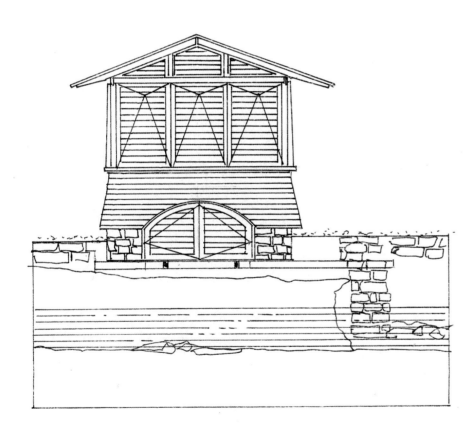

LEFT AND TOP | Aboriginal carvings and nineteenth-century graffiti mark the sandstone rock shelf, evidence of the site's appeal over the centuries.

ABOVE | East elevation, facing the water's edge.

RIGHT | Plan of the first floor.

TWENTY-FIRST-CENTURY BOATHOUSES

FUSSACH BOOTSHAUS

FUSSACH, VORARLBERG, AUSTRIA (2000)

Lake Constance (Bodensee to the Germans) lies between Austria, Germany and Switzerland in the heart of central Europe. The town of Fussach is at the lake's southeastern tip. During the 1960s a network of canals was dug, integrating the lake with the town centre. In the subsequent decades the canal banks have been colonized by residential boathouses; weekend getaways for boating enthusiasts.

Most of the houses are informal, low-key affairs, typically making reference to alpine hut vernacular, and generally with the emphasis on the comfort of the boats as opposed to the occupants on the upper levels. The latest addition, an abstract metal-sheathed house designed by architect brothers Stefan and Bernhard Marte, marks a distinct stylistic departure.

The architects took advantage of local planning regulations, which specify only site boundaries, roof pitches and building heights, to improvise with openings and materials. The timber-framed *bootshaus* has a skin of riveted aluminium panels, which is distinguished to the west and east by full-height windows. A kitchen and dining area, as well as three compact bedrooms and a bathroom, are accommodated on this first floor. A fold-down staircase concealed in the ceiling leads to the roof space, which features two 10ft x 13ft/3m x 4m flaps that can be opened to create an open-air terrace with views of Lake Constance. The staircase and roof flaps are operated hydraulically, a reference to the client's profession manufacturing body parts for trucks.

Access to the double-height two-boat wet dock and storage area is via a discreet door in the north elevation. A 23ft/7m-wide door slides back to offer access to the canal, and to Lake Constance beyond.

FAR LEFT | A seven metre wide door opens on to the canal, which links Fussach to Lake Constance.

ABOVE | The abstract aluminium-sheathed *bootshaus* is in marked contrast to its alpine vernacular neighbours.

LEFT | Two hydraulically operated roof flaps open to create a terrace with views of Lake Constance.

ABOVE | View from the living space. The colony of canal-side boathouses has evolved since the 1960s.

RIGHT | Plan of first floor.

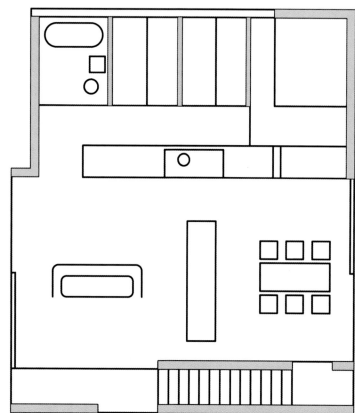

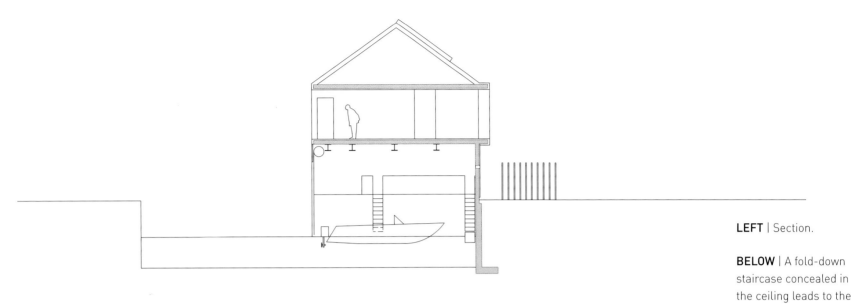

LEFT | Section.

BELOW | A fold-down staircase concealed in the ceiling leads to the roof space.

LAKE AUSTIN BOAT DOCK

AUSTIN, TEXAS, USA (2000)

Architects Juan Miró and Miguel Rivera were given free rein to design a boathouse for private use at the bottom of a steep bluff on Lake Austin. Their response to the open brief was an inventive reinterpretation of standard boathouse typologies, in terms of plan, form and materials.

The two level building makes minimum impact, both visually and environmentally. It is nestled in a natural recess in the shoreline and surrounded by mature trees. To reduce its bulk, the two wet docks are parallel to the shoreline, as opposed to projecting out into the lake. The lower level also accommodates a jet-ski slip and storage space. A staircase at the rear leads to the upper level sun deck.

The Boat Dock consists of a structural frame of steel I-beams and steel tube piles drilled into the lake bed. A screen of 3.5-inch by 1.5-inch steel tubes spaced 1.5 inches apart forms a screen on the lake-facing elevation. Ipe decking on the upper level extends towards the shore, with built-in benches and a table shielded from the sun by a fabric canopy stretched with masts and tensioning cables. The canopy is independent of the main steel frame. The white fabric, stretched by masts and tensioning masts, is a reference to the sailing boats that use the lake.

To the southeast a ramp leads to an electric tram that links the Boat Dock to the house at the top of the hill: the green painted steel tram carriage is camouflaged on the hill. The only other means of access is from the lake itself.

Miró Rivera Architects won numerous awards for the scheme. It also won the practice another commission, the 'Manyana Boat Dock' on the opposite side of the lake.

LEFT | The Boat Dock is parallel to the shore. The two boat slips face each other, with openings at each end.

RIGHT | Nestled in a natural recess and composed of lightweight materials, the Boat Dock makes minimal impact on its environment.

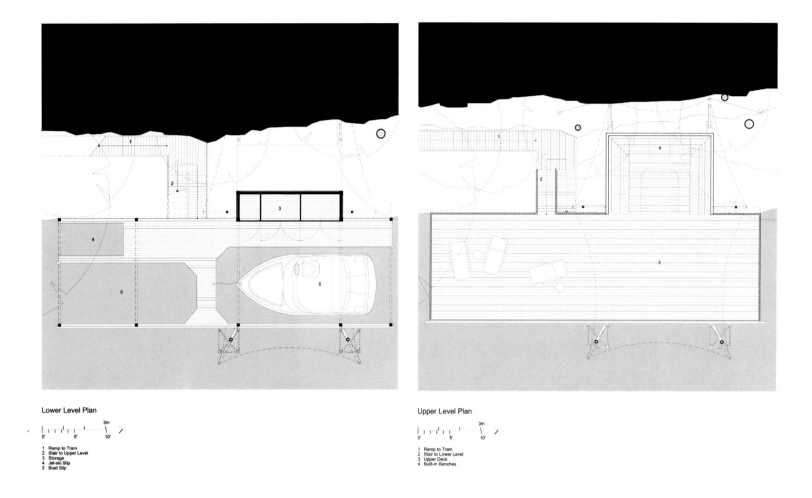

Lower Level Plan

```
        3m
|  |  |  |  |      >
0'    5'    10'
```

1 Ramp to Tram
2 Stair to Upper Level
3 Storage
4 Jet-ski Slip
5 Boat Slip

Upper Level Plan

```
        3m
|  |  |  |  |      >
0'    5'    10'
```

1 Ramp to Tram
2 Stair to Lower Level
3 Upper Deck
4 Built-in Benches

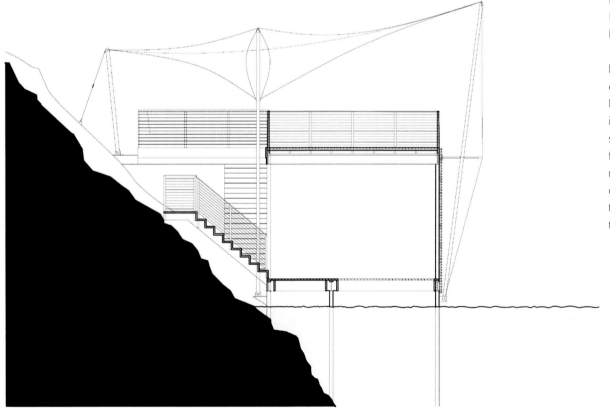

LEFT | Section: The Boat Dock is at the bottom of a steep bluff.

RIGHT | The canopy, enclosing the upper level deck space, is independent of the main steel frame. The white fabric, stretched by masts and tensioning cables, is a reference to the sailing boats that use the lake.

MINNEAPOLIS ROWING CLUB

MINNEAPOLIS, USA (2001)

Like Eadweard Muybridge's use of freeze-frame photography to distil the dynamics of motion, architect Vincent James based the roof profile of the Minneapolis Rowing Club on analysis of the movement of oars through water. The resulting hyperbolic paraboloid form lends a sense of dynamism to the building's otherwise austere envelope.

The Minneapolis Rowing Club is a private, not-for-profit organization that depends on membership fees and volunteer support for survival. The present boathouse, on an isolated site close to the Lake Street Bridge in the Mississippi Gorge, is its second base. The original Duncan-Miller boathouse, built by the club members over a six-year period, was destroyed in an arson attack in 1997.

James, a Minneapolis-based architect, was commissioned to work with the club on a replacement facility. The budget was tight, and planning requirements defined a long narrow building. Design considerations included the use of common, inexpensive materials; bringing club members into the construction process; practical issues related to the storage, movement and maintenance of boats; and the design of a building that was resistant to fire and vandalism.

The uniform envelope is composed of shiplap cementitious board painted black and laid horizontally to the frame. This is punctuated with copper-clad sliding doors and copper corner reveals. Clerestory windows of polycarbonate glazing allow light into the main double-height volume, and the mezzanine level. The wave-like roof form was generated by the incremental rotation of the inverted timber and steel cable trusses around an axis that runs the length of the building.

The building was completed at a cost of only US$600,000.

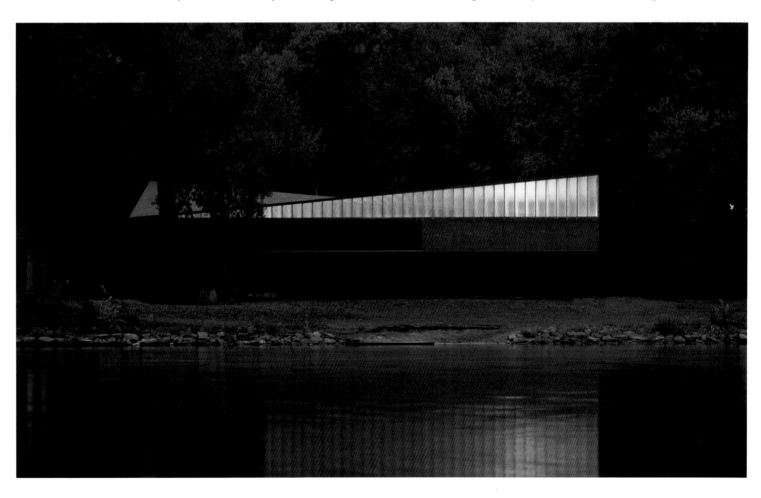

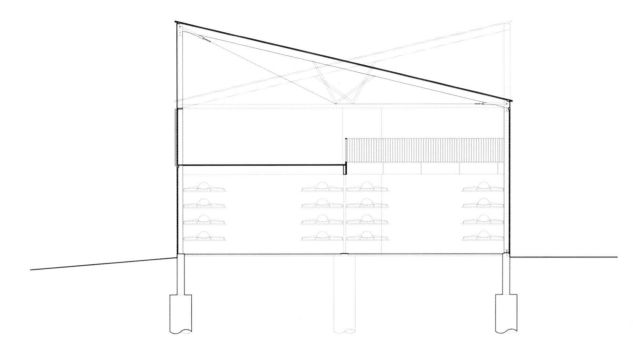

FAR LEFT | Freeze-frame photography of oars moving through water was the inspiration for the wave-like roof profile of the Minneapolis Rowing Club.

LEFT | Section through the rowing club.

BELOW | Clerestory windows and copper doors animate the exterior.

ABOVE | The roof form is created by the incremental rotation of the inverted trusses.

ABOVE RIGHT | View of the Lake Street Bridge from the mezzanine level.

RIGHT | Common, low-cost materials were used to minimize the budget.

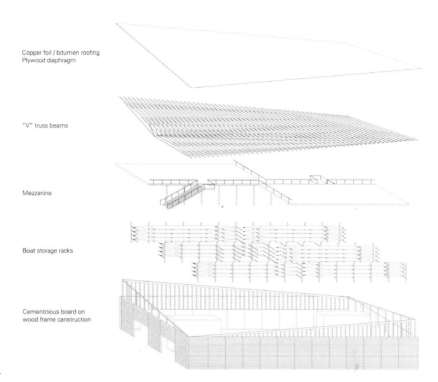

Copper foil / bitumen roofing
Plywood diaphragm

"V" truss beams

Mezzanine

Boat storage racks

Cementitious board on
wood frame canstruction

RIGHT | Cutaway axonometric.

MUSKOKA BOATHOUSE

LAKE MUSKOKA, ONTARIO, CANADA (2001)

FAR LEFT | The Muskoka Boathouse strikes a balance between contemporary and vernacular traditions in the wilderness setting.

LEFT | The outer shell is formed by timber boards laid vertically and horizontally.

BELOW | Ground floor plan.

were removed and the cribs fell to the lake's granite base. Rocks were dropped into the cribs, to hold them in place. It is a technique that has long been used in the Ontario lakes.

Although hidden from view beneath the water, the building's primitive foundations are expressed in the heavy timber boards, laid horizontally, that form its protective outer shell. Interior finishes combine ordinary and sophisticated materials: cabinets with Douglas fir plywood panels and intricate mahogany windows, each detailed to allow differential settlement from movement in the crib foundations.

The Muskoka Boathouse is located on the southwestern shore of Lake Muskoka, a two-hour drive north of Toronto. In form, materials and structural system it is a response to both the pre-Cambrian granite that makes up the bedrock of Ontario's lakes and forests, and the local aesthetic of pioneer log cabins, Victorian cottages and hand-crafted timber boats. In developing the concept for the boathouse, architects Brigitte Shim and Howard Sutcliffe also referred to the work of the Group of Seven, painters who portrayed the wild and romantic landscape while canoeing through the region in the early twentieth century.

The building comprises one outdoor and two indoor slips, as well as a bedroom, sitting room, bathrooms and a cabin with kitchenette. There are also several porches and terraces, and a moss garden planted with local species.

The building straddles the boundary between the thick mixed forest and Lake Muskoka. Construction of the submerged foundations on the lake-facing (northeast) side began during the winter. The first stage involved drawing the outlines of the three boat slips on the frozen lake surface, and using chainsaws to cut away holes. Sleepers were then laid across the holes while 'cribs', square timber boxes that form the building's underwater infrastructure, were erected on top. Once complete, the sleepers

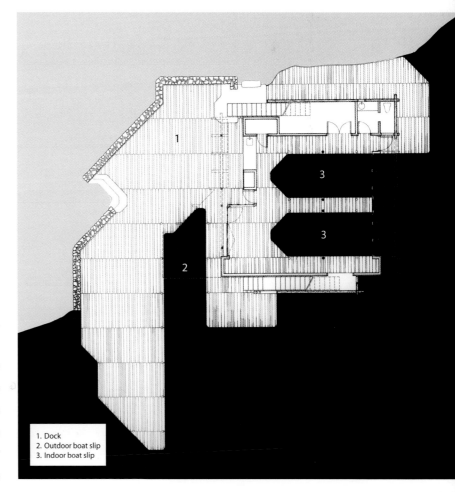

1. Dock
2. Outdoor boat slip
3. Indoor boat slip

LEFT | The boathouse comprises one outdoor and two enclosed slips. Outlines of the three boat slips were drawn on the frozen lake surface. Chainsaws were used to cut away holes.

ABOVE | One of the lake-level terraces.

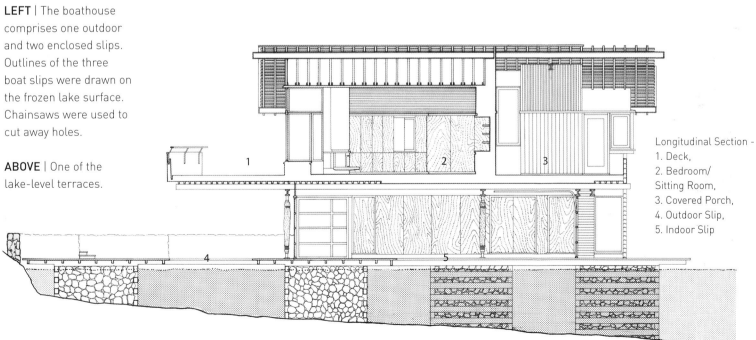

Longitudinal Section -
1. Deck,
2. Bedroom/ Sitting Room,
3. Covered Porch,
4. Outdoor Slip,
5. Indoor Slip

LEFT, BELOW AND RIGHT | Internal finishes are a combination of sophisticated (mahogany) and ordinary (plywood) materials.

MARITIME YOUTH HOUSE

SUNDBY HARBOUR, COPENHAGEN, DENMARK (2004)

The Maritime Youth House was designed for joint occupants, a youth club and a yacht club. Its form is a synthesis of their requirements. The undulating timber deck creates a safe, secure play space for children to run, skateboard and cycle. The raised areas beneath the deck are used for boat storage. There is also communal space for meetings and administration.

The building occupies a contaminated former industrial site in Sundby Harbour, close to Copenhagen. Initially, it was anticipated that around 25 per cent of the budget would be required for site remediation works. Analysis later revealed that the sub-soil contamination was caused by heavy metals,

which were stable if left undisturbed. So the architects, the Bjarke Ingels Group (BIG), developed a strategy that would enable 100 per cent of the available funds to be invested in the new structure.

Instead of digging down, BIG designed a light, low impact deck, square in plan, whose weight is spread across the building's 49 timber piles. The heights of the piles differ to create the ripple-effect timber deck. The cavities underneath the undulations also created nooks and crannies for the storage of boats and sailing equipment. It was a simple low-cost solution that met the objectives of both clients.

LEFT AND BELOW |
The Maritime Youth
House occupies a
former industrial
site on a harbour
outside Copenhagen.

RIGHT AND BELOW |
The square deck is
carried on 49 timber
piles of varying lengths,
to create the ripple-
effect timber deck.

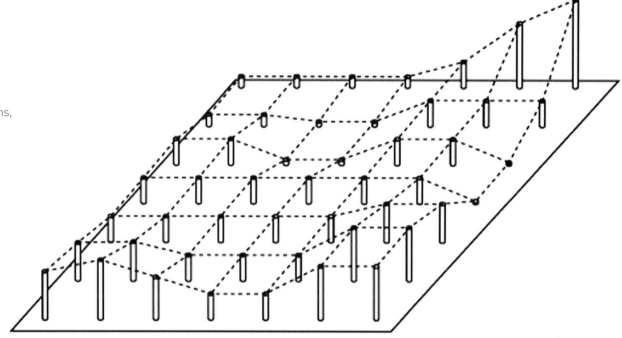

AOVE AND RIGHT |
Enclosed areas
underneath the deck
include a common
room and space for
boat storage.

CENTRE D'INTERPRETATION DU CANAL

POUILLY-EN-AUXOIS, BURGUNDY, FRANCE (2004)

Japanese architect Shigeru Ban (born 1957) has built his reputation on the structural application of recycled paper tubes. It began as a response to budgetary limitations – a 1986 exhibition installation of Alvar Aalto's furniture and glass in Tokyo was the first time he used paper tubes – but the qualities of the material as thermally efficient, environmentally sustainable, versatile and extremely strong quickly came to the fore.

Since the early-1990s, Ban's buildings using compressed paper as columns and structural framing include libraries, theatres, churches, emergency shelters for victims of natural and man-made disasters and pavilions for international exhibitions. The barge shelter at the Centre d'Interpretation du Canal in Burgundy was one of his first European projects.

The shelter is part of the first phase of a cultural complex dedicated to the history of the Canal de Bourgogne. The canal, built between the 1720s and 1830s, is a feat of engineering that links the Atlantic Ocean to the Mediterranean Sea via the Yonne, Seine, Saône and Rhône rivers. At 1,240ft/378m above sea level, the small town of Pouilly-en-Auxois is the highest point on the 150 mile (240km) canal system. The canal traverses Pouilly in an underground tunnel.

The transparent arched structure is composed of a triangular latticework grid of compressed paper tubes. The frame is enclosed in ribbed plastic sheeting. The frame, which is carried on metal footings set in a concrete base, is 100ft/30.5m long and 18ft 4in/5.6m wide and reaches a height of 38ft/11.5m at its apex, allowing plenty of room for visitors to walk around the historic barge.

The first phase of the Centre d'Interpretation du Canal also includes a single-storey glazed pavilion, which accommodates the entrance lobby, shop and exhibition space. Transparency is a key feature of both the pavilion and barge shelter, ensuring that their conspicuously contemporary forms sit unobtrusively in the rustic, semi-rural setting.

LEFT | Shigeru Ban's paper tube buildings are a happy marriage of high design and strong environmental credentials.

BELOW | The paper tubes are fixed to six-pronged die-cast aluminium joints.

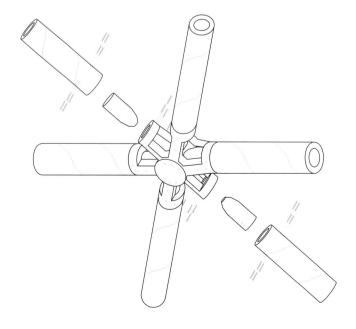

ABOVE | The Centre d'Interpretation du Canal is dedicated to the canal network that links the Atlantic to the Mediterranean. The first phase comprises the barge shelter and a glazed pavilion.

PORTER BOATHOUSE

UNIVERSITY OF WISCONSIN, USA (2005)

LEFT | The Porter
boathouse is the third
at the University of
Wisconsin since
the 1890s.

BELOW | Site plan.

BOTTOM | The saw-
tooth roof illuminates
the upper level.

There is a long and proud tradition of rowing at the University of Wisconsin. United States teams at every Olympiad between 1968 and 2000 featured Wisconsin rowers. The university has an equally impressive tradition of boathouses.

The first, completed in 1893, was an elaborate Shingle Style structure distinguished by a corner tower used as a lifeguard lookout. At the beginning of the twentieth century there was talk of Frank Lloyd Wright designing a boathouse for the university. This building eventually saw the light of day in Buffalo in 2007 (see pages 88–91).

The 1893 boathouse was replaced by a single-storey concrete structure in 1967. But while rowing standards were unaffected, the new premises were cramped and little loved. The present boathouse, designed by Vincent James (see also Minneapolis Rowing Club, pages 128–131), is a far more salubrious affair.

The building occupies the site of its predecessor at the end of Babcock Drive, in the heart of the university campus. It provides 51,667sqft/4,800sqm of space over three floors.

The main entrance is on the first floor, which also includes offices, locker rooms, a rowing tank for winter practice, kitchen and medical facilities, as well as historic displays and the rowers' 'hall of fame'. The ground floor, raised two feet higher than its predecessor to minimize the threat of flooding, includes storage space for over 100 boats, and a boat repair bay. Training facilities and an external terrace facing the lake are accommodated on the third floor.

The building exterior is a tripartite stratification of materials. On the top level, three steel trusses span the width of the building (79ft/24m), to create a vaulted clerestory window for the training facilities below. The solid areas of the roof are clad in lead-coated copper. The first floor is sheathed in limestone, to respond to the neighbouring dormitory buildings. The ground floor storage level is cast *in situ* in concrete.

Vincent James Architects Associates designed the boathouse in collaboration with KEE Architecture Inc, of Madison.

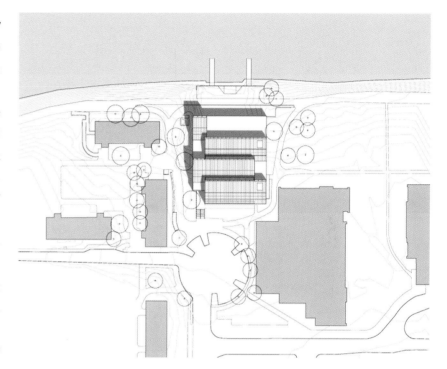

TENBY LIFEBOAT STATIONS

TENBY, PEMBROKESHIRE (1905 AND 2005)

The present lifeboat house at Tenby, a picturesque port with a large tidal range on Wales' treacherous south coast, is the fourth in the town since the 1850s. Lifesaving technology and the scale and capability of lifeboats have changed almost beyond recognition since then.

The first of Tenby's lifeboat houses, located in Penniless Cove, was built to accommodate a ten-oared self-righting lifeboat provided by the Shipwrecked Fishermen and Mariners' Benevolent Society in 1852. Both the boat and boathouse were replaced in the early-1860s. The new boathouse was a stone structure with a pitched roof raised on a podium connected to Castle Beach by a timber slipway. It was built to house RNLB *Florence*.

In 1904, the anticipated introduction of a motor-powered launch led to another upgrade, this time a radical new approach intended to overcome the problem of Tenby's tidal range. The new boathouse, near the site of the now demolished Royal Victoria Pier, was a slipway launch facility in which the lifeboat house was carried on piles in the sea, with a steep slip stretching into the water.

There are a number of advantages to slipway launch boathouses: the boat can be kept safely out of the water and launched relatively easily in virtually any conditions. Disadvantages include returning to the slipway in poor weather, and protecting the propellers from damage on the slipway.

The boathouse itself was a relatively lightweight structure, a timber frame clad in corrugated sheet metal, giving it the appearance of an industrial shed.

RIGHT | Tenby, a picturesque port in the Pembrokeshire National Park, is located on a treacherous stretch of the Welsh coast.

LEFT | The second of Tenby's four lifeboat stations was built in the 1860s next to Castle Beach.

BELOW | Economy and lightweight materials are features of the 1904 lifeboat house.

RIGHT | The present £5.5m lifeboat station includes crew and public facilities unimaginable in its predecessors.

As it turned out, the motor-powered lifeboat did not arrive until 1923. The Watson-Class RNLB *John R Webb* required no oars or sails. Its 80hp engine pushed the boat along at 8.6 knots. However, it was 45ft x 12ft 6/00 x 00 m, which required a £10,000 upgrade of the boathouse to accommodate it.

The present boathouse was completed in 2005. Like its predecessor, also on the north shore of Castle Hill, the new facility is a slipway boathouse. The £5.5m structure was built to house a new Tamar class lifeboat, a £2m vessel with a top speed of 25 knots. It is much larger and more salubrious that the 1905 boathouse, including toilets and meeting rooms for the crew, and a viewing platform and a shop selling merchandise for visitors.

Building the boathouse was a challenge. The site is inaccessible by road, and dray lorries carrying beer to the pubs are the largest vehicles permitted into the town, so most of the building materials were brought by sea and construction undertaken from a large jack-up barge. The exception was concrete that was pumped several hundred yards from the nearest road head with police enforcing parking restrictions in Tenby's narrow streets to ensure access.

PLINIO TORNO SPORTS CLUB

LAKE COMO, ITALY (2006)

To the 600 residents of Torno, a small village north of Milan on the southwest arm of Lake Como, rowing is a way of life. Over half of them are members of the Plinio Torno Sports Club. So towards the end of the 1990s, when it became clear that the club's makeshift boathouse was no longer fit for purpose, the search for a solution was a matter of village-wide debate.

Turin-based architects Michele Bonino and Subhash Mukerjee – themselves keen rowers – were asked to visit the proposed site and discuss design ideas. Their brief was for a new boat storage facility with attached changing rooms on the site of the existing boathouse, on the western edge of the village square.

Bonino and Mukerjee recommended that the boathouse be 'sunk' into a small cove to the side of the site, next to a brick-built 1950s lakefront villa – the first complete work of famed architects Attilio and Carlo Terragni. That way the roof of the new structure would project only one metre above the floor level of the square, and views of the lake and mountains would not be interrupted.

The owner of the 1950s lakefront villa donated about two-thirds of the estimated cost (€100,000); his family was one of the co-founders of the sports club. The remaining €30,000 was generated by contributions from other members. Those unable to contribute money offered their services as carpenters and labourers, to help minimize costs and speed construction.

The building is composed of two distinct elements: the main body comprising the changing rooms and storeroom, which sits in the cove; and the two lightweight shed-like volumes that project out over the lake. The roof of the boathouse, accessed via a short ramp from the village square, forms a new belvedere, with beautiful views of Lake Como and the surrounding mountains.

RIGHT | The small Plinio Torno Sports Club boathouse sits in a natural creek sloping down to the edge of Lake Como.

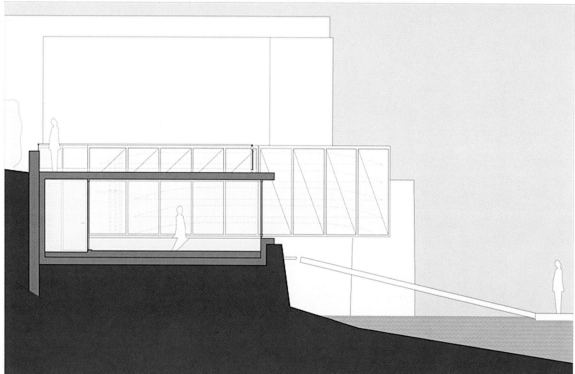

The use of translucent materials in the steel-framed boat storage elements – Including shockproof honeycomb Plexiglas and tarpaulin – creates an impression of impermanence, but there is nothing short-term about the Plinio Torno boathouse. It is flood proof and all components carry a guarantee of at least 20 years. An additional benefit is that the boathouse creates a particularly pleasing effect at night, when the water of the lake is reflected in the translucent walls and the extended boat store becomes an object suspended between the land and the water.

Michele Bonino and Subhash Mukerjee are now working on a refurbishment to and extension of the Reale Società Canottieri Cerea on the River Po in Turin, the boathouse and headquarters of Italy's oldest rowing club (see pages 76–77).

LEFT | Section west-east (top) and east elevation (below) show how the boathouse has been integrated into the shape of the shoreline.

BELOW | A belvedere on the roof of the changing rooms and office space is linked to the village square by a shallow ramp.

BOTTOM | Lightweight but resilient materials were used in the construction of the boat store, including shockproof Plexiglass, tarpaulin and a steel frame.

CHESAPEAKE BOATHOUSE

OKLAHOMA CITY, OKLAHOMA, USA (2006)

Materials used in the construction of contemporary rowing sculls include carbon fibre, fibreglass and Kevlar, with raw aluminium outrigger frames and lightweight oars. They are strong, lightweight and elegant. Architect Rand Elliott took the streamlined modernity of the twenty-first century scull as inspiration for the Chesapeake Boathouse, a slender, steel-framed structure wrapped in a translucent polycarbonate skin with a roof of white standing-seam metal.

The elliptical plan form is a metaphor for a rowing shell, with the 'bow' at the western end. The entrance to the southwest is defined by a row of sixteen steel pylons representing oars. Public areas and administration are located to the west of the building interior. The central portion is dedicated to a large boat store capable of accommodating 124 boats, ranging from single sculls to eight-person shells. Changing rooms, fitness and boat repair facilities are to the east.

When completed in 2006, the 14,530sq ft/1,350sqm boathouse was the first building on the banks of the revitalized Oklahoma River. Previously an under-developed barrier between the north and south of Oklahoma City, the river has been repositioned as a central unifying component by a US$56million urban regeneration programme.

Elliott was commissioned to design the boathouse by the non-profit-making Oklahoma City Boathouse Foundation, a body formed to oversee its management and operation for junior, adult and collegiate rowers.

Following the success of the Chesapeake Boathouse, both as a civic landmark and sports facility, approval was granted for a further three boathouses on the Oklahoma River, all designed by Rand Elliott. Unsurprisingly, there are plans to name it 'Boathouse Row' (see pages 70–71).

RIGHT | Oklahoma City's 'Core to Shore' urban regeneration initiative seeks to establish the Oklahoma River as a unifying component of the city centre.

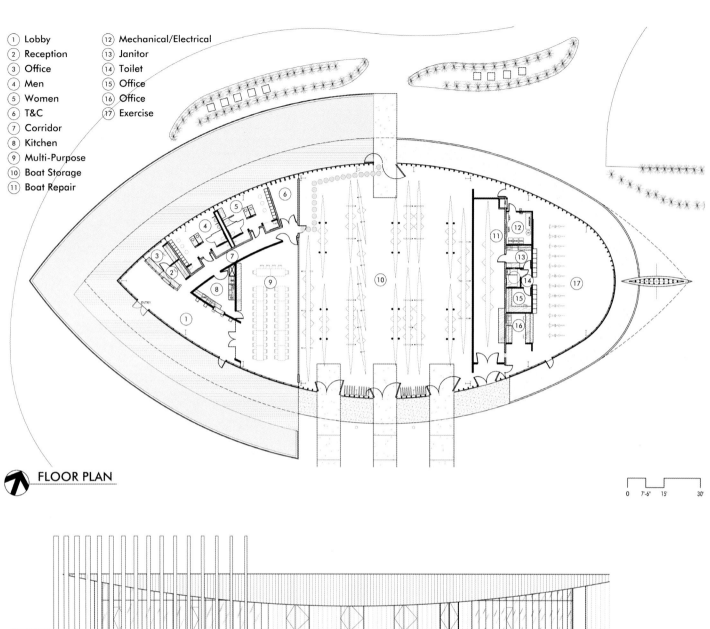

1. Lobby
2. Reception
3. Office
4. Men
5. Women
6. T&C
7. Corridor
8. Kitchen
9. Multi-Purpose
10. Boat Storage
11. Boat Repair
12. Mechanical/Electrical
13. Janitor
14. Toilet
15. Office
16. Office
17. Exercise

FLOOR PLAN

0   7'-6"   15'   30'

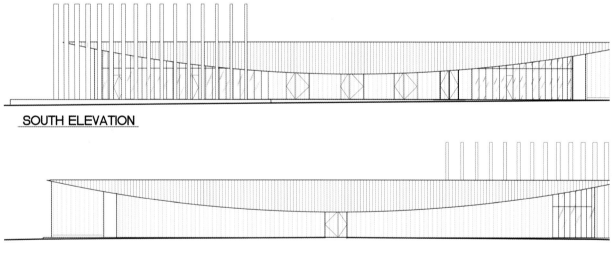

SOUTH ELEVATION

NORTH ELEVATION

EAST ELEVATION   WEST ELEVATION

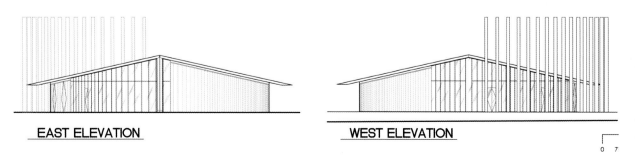

RIGHT | Sixteen concave steel pylons, representing oars, mark the main entrance at the 'bow' of the boathouse.

0   7

LUNA ROSSA TEAM BASE

VALENCIA, SPAIN (2007)

BELOW | A sketch of the
cladding system
by Renzo Piano.

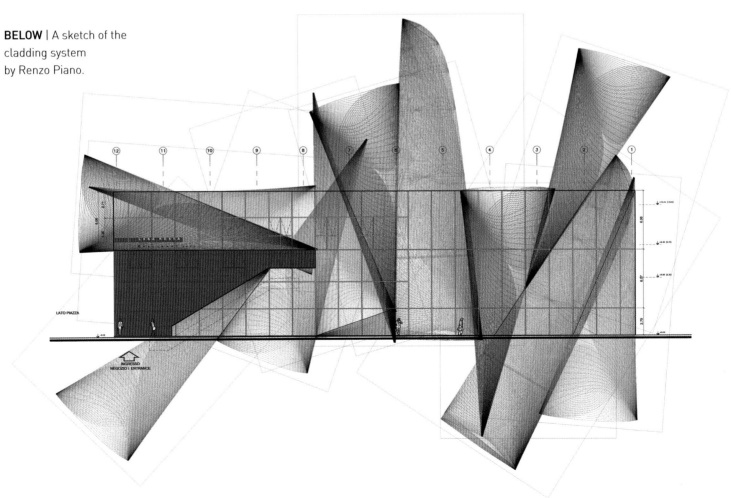

Team Alinghi from landlocked Switzerland won the 2003 America's Cup. The result meant that in 2007, for the first time since 1851, the America's Cup would be contested in Europe. Team Alinghi's search for a suitable coastal city from which to host its defence led to Valencia, whose historic waterfront was given a facelift to mark the occasion: English architect David Chipperfield designed the Veles e Vents spectator building, the Port Authority building was renovated and Genoese architect Renzo Piano was commissioned to work on the Prada team's operating base.

Piano's contribution to the three-storey steel-framed building was the cladding system, a semi-translucent patchwork of 50 recycled Kevlar sails accumulated from *Luna Rossa's* two previous runs for the America's Cup, arranged in 485 panels and covering a total area of 33,368sqft/3,100sqm. The sails were preassembled on aluminium frames and erected in only 40 days. To improve the cladding's technical performance, particularly resistance to high winds, the Kevlar was reinforced with polycarbonate. The effect is distinctively collage-like. At night the building glows; during the day the Kevlar filters natural light.

The ground floor of the building measures a little over 21,528sqft/2,000sqm and comprises the workshop and storage area for masts and sails. Sails are hung from a full-height vertical column, to enable washing. The two upper levels accommodate offices, dining areas, sleeping space and the team gym. A terrace at the top of the building offers panoramic views of the docks.

FLOATING BOATHOUSE

LAKE HURON, POINTE AU BARIL, ONTARIO, CANADA (2007)

The Great Lakes region is well known to the Worples; the Cincinnati-based couple had spent their summer holidays in the region for years. So when the opportunity came up to buy a three-acre island in the northeast of Lake Huron, it was too good an opportunity to miss.

The outcrop of pink-tinged granite, 20 minutes by boat to the mainland, was home to two ageing cottages and a two-storey over-water boathouse, all of which were in poor condition. Architects Michael Meredith and Hilary Sample (MOS Architects) proposed to replace them with new low-impact buildings suited to the scenic and exposed setting. The Floating Boathouse is the second in the series, following a two-bedroom cottage (2005).

The footprint of the existing boathouse meant that a new boathouse was permitted within the cove of the horseshoe-shaped island. The decision to carry the new building on pontoons was driven by two practical considerations. One related to the environment: annual cyclical change compounded by global environmental trends cause the level of Lake Huron to vary significantly from month-to-month and year-to-year; a boat-house carried on the water's surface can adapt to these changes. The other reason was financial. If the boathouse had been built using

LEFT | The Floating Boathouse occupies the footprint of a dilapidated two-storey predecessor on an isolated island in Lake Huron.

conventional methods, the cost of transporting materials, tradespeople and machinery to the site would have swallowed up much of the budget. Instead, the steel platform with incorporated pontoons was towed to the contractor's lakeside workshop, where the superstructure was built. The house was then towed to the site and anchored. In total, the boathouse travelled approximately 50miles/80km across the lake during the various construction stages.

The ground floor of the gabled roof structure comprises a wet dock open to the lake, a sauna and storage, with a large west-facing living area, two bedrooms, kitchen and office above. Two timber bridges link the house to the island: one on the south elevation, leading from the first floor towards the cottage, the other on the north, at ground level. Both the boathouse and the cottage are clad in raw cedar, to harmonize with the landscape.

ABOVE | The boathouse is connected to the island by a timber bridge at the first floor level.

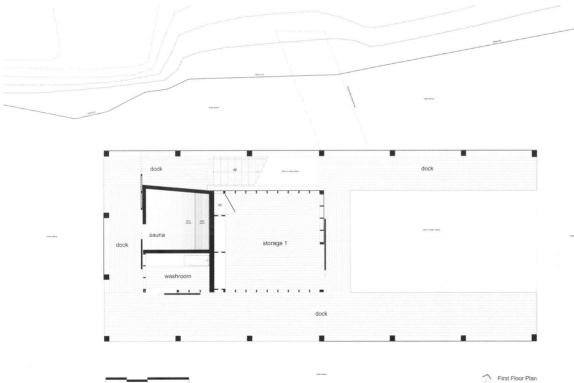

First Floor Plan

ABOVE | The Floating Boathouse is one of a series of low-impact, cedar-clad structures designed for the island. The first was a two-bedroom cottage.

LEFT | A first floor plan. A wet dock, open to the lake, faces east.

LOUISE-CATHERINE GALLERY

QUAI D'AUSTERLITZ, PARIS, FRANCE

A former coal barge is to be adapted as a Paris art gallery. While the works are underway a sculptural ribbon of profiled aluminium will shield the barge from public view. It is the latest chapter in the extraordinary story of the *Louise-Catherine*.

The ferro-concrete barge (230ft x 26ft/70m x 8m) was built in around 1919, to transport coal from Le Havre to Paris. Like all the barges in the convoy, it was not motorized. Tugboats drew it along the waterways of northeast France. But the working life of 'Liege' barge number P9403F was brief. Within less than a decade it was surplus to requirements.

In 1929, the French Salvation Army was looking for premises for a 'Floating Asylum' as a refuge for Parisian vagrants during the winter months. In March of that year their search took them north to Rouen, where they found barge P9403F.

ABOVE | The sculptural ribbon of profiled aluminium was designed to shield views of the *Louise-Catherine* while she is converted to a gallery.

RIGHT | The shield is composed of three modules. The dimensions of each module differ, creating a ripple effect accentuated by the reflection of the river. The aluminium shield is carried on pontoons.

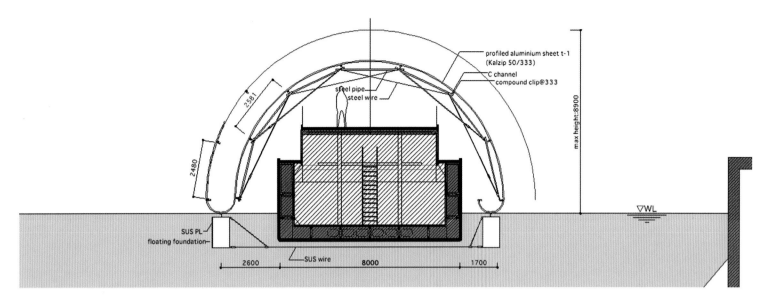

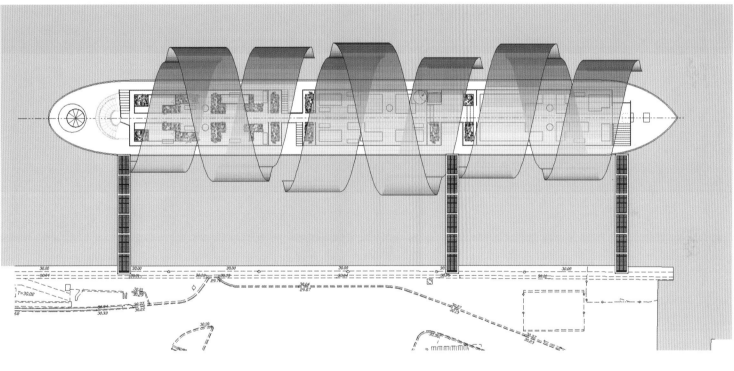

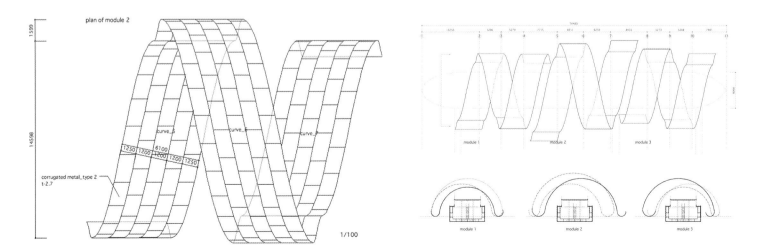

BELOW | A lithograph published in the Salvation Army bulletin in 1930. The article described the history of the *Louise-Catherine* and her conversion to a 'Floating Asylum'.

With funding from the Ministry of Labour, supplemented by backing from Princess Singer de Polignac, a long-time benefactor of the Salvation Army and contemporary artists, the barge was acquired and transported to Paris. There it was renamed the *Louise-Catherine*, in honour of the recently deceased artist Louise-Catherine Breslau whose partner Madeleine Zillhardt had originally hatched the idea for the 'Floating Asylum', and converted into a dormitory by Le Corbusier. At the time, the guru of the Modern Movement was also working on La Villa Savoye, one of the landmarks of Modern architecture.

The *Louise-Catherine* was completely transformed. A floor was inserted at the bottom of the holds, windows were cut along both sides, a concrete deck was built to enclose the three large dormitories and bridges were built to connect the barge to the riverbank. She was also fitted out with showers, a kitchen and a refectory, which doubled as a meeting room.

The *Louise-Catherine* was used as a refuge until World War II, when she was refitted for military use. Subsequent phases of alteration and modification mean that almost no fabric dating to the Le Corbusier fit-out survives.

Early in the twenty-first century, by then in a state of partial dereliction, the *Louise-Catherine* was acquired for conversion to an art gallery, to a design by Paris architect ACYC. The prominence of the barge at Quai d'Austerlitz on the Seine, and the lengthy nature of the construction works prompted the gallery to consider an innovative approach to maintaining the appearance of the *Louise-Catherine*.

Shuhei Endo, a Japanese architect noted for his sculptural application of sheet metal, has been invited to design a shield, to screen views of the barge while construction is underway. Endo's solution is three modules of profiled aluminium sheeting supported on a frame of steel pipe and wire and carried on pontoons. It will be prefabricated down river and floated into position. The modules form an undulating arch over the barge. It is a work of art in its own right.

BIBLIOGRAPHY

Books
Anderson, Stanford, *Peter Behrens and a New Architecture for the 20th Century*, MIT Press, Cambridge, Massachusetts, 2000.

Anonymous, *The House Book*, Phaidon, London, 2001.

Anonymous, *The Phaidon Atlas of Contemporary World Architecture*, Phaidon, London, 2006.

Anonymous (Introduction by David Buck), *Shigeru Ban*, GG portfolio, Barcelona, 1997.

Bachrach, Julia Sniderman, *The City in a Garden: A Photographic History of Chicago's Parks,* The Center for American Places, Chicago, 2001.

Beard, Geoffrey, *The Work of Robert Adam*, Bloomsbury Books, London, 1978.

Bolton, Arthur T., *The Architecture of Robert and James Adam (1758–1794)*, volumes I and II, Country Life, London, 1922.

Christie, Agatha, *Dead Man's Folly*, William Collins Sons & Co. Ltd., London, 1956.

Dugard, Martin, *Farther Than Any Man: The Rise and Fall of Captain James Cook*, Pocket Books, New York, 2001.

Hamilton, Jill Duchess of and Julia Bruce, *The Flower Chain: The Early Discovery of Australian Plants*, Kangaroo Press, East Roseville, New South Wales, 1998.

Hawkesworth, John, *An Account of the Voyages for making discoveries in the Southern Hemisphere*, volumes I, II and III, W. Strahan & T. Cadell, London, 1773.

Hill, Barry, *The Enduring Rip: A History of Queenscliffe*, Melbourne University Press, Carlton, Victoria, 2004.

Howarth, Patrick, *The Life-Boat Story*, Routledge and Kegan Paul, London, 1957.

Kadatz, Hans-Joachim, *Peter Behrens Künstlerkompendium,* VEB E. A. Seemann Verlag, Leipzig, 1977.

Kowsky, Francis R., *Country, Park and City: The Architecture and Life of Calvert Vaux*, Oxford University Press, New York and Oxford, 1998.

Sharp, Dennis and Sally Rendel, *Connell, Ward and Lucas*, Frances Lincoln, London, 2008.

Thomas, Aeronwy, *A Daughter Remembers Dylan*, Merton Books, London, 2006.

Trencher, Michael, *The Alvar Aalto Guide*, Princeton Architectural Press, New York, 1996.

Turner, Tom, *Garden History, Philosophy and Design 2000BC–2000AD*, Spon Press, London, 2005.

Uglow, Jenny, *A Little History of British Gardening*, Pimlico, London, 2005.

Weston, Richard, *Alvar Aalto*, Phaidon, London, 1995.

Windsor, Alan, *Peter Behrens: Architect and Designer*, Architectural Press, London, 1981.

Articles
The Builder, 22 May 1875, pp. 462–3.

The Builder, 15 September 1883, p. 361–3.

Civil Engineer and Architect's Journal, August 1858, pp. 278–9.

Harris, Eileen and Alastair Laing, 'No Fishy Tale: A true account of the Fishing Room at Kedleston', *Apollo*, 1 April 2006.

Holzhueter, John O., 'Cudworth Beye, Frank Lloyd Wright and the Yahara Boathouse, 1905', *Journal of the Taliesin Fellows*, issue 20, Winter 1996.

Moore, Rowan, 'It's made of paper but built to last', *London Evening Standard*, 20 March 2001.

Skempton, Professor A.W., 'The Boat Store, Sheerness (1858–60) and its Place in Structural History', *Transactions of the Newcomen Society*, volume XXXII, 1959–60, p. 59.

Skempton, Professor A.W. and Eric de Maré, 'The Sheerness Boat Store', *RIBA Journal*, volume 68, 1961, pp. 318–24.

Wise, M. Norton and Elaine M. Wise, 'Reform in the garden', *Endeavour*, Volume 26 (4), 2002.

Unpublished reports
Bachrach, Julia and Ellen Berkelhamer, Historic District Nomination form for Humboldt Park, Chicago, National Register of Historic Places, US Dept. of the Interior, National Park Service, 1992.

Hunter, Andrew, 'Lifeboat Houses: The History and Development of Lifeboat Houses of the Royal National Lifeboat Institution', unpublished thesis, Architectural Association, London, 1996.

Websites
learn.bowdoin.edu/japanesegardens

Simons, Chaim, 'Seven Years at Carmel College: Reminiscences of a Pupil 1953–60', 2004, geocities.com/CapitolHill/Senate/7854/carmelcollege.html

'South Sea: Voyaging and Cross-Cultural Encounters in the Pacific (1760–1800)', southseas.nla.gov.au

www.andrewcusack.com/blog/2007/01/argentinas_henl.php

www.trevarno.co.uk

ACKNOWLEDGEMENTS

Julia Sniderman Bachrach, historian of the Chicago Park District, USA (see also bibliography)

Joanne Bauer, Senior Principal BauerLatoza Studio, Chicago, USA

Michele Bonino, MARC Studio, Italy

Amiral François Célérier, Société Nationale de Sauvetage en Mer, France

Sharon Courtin, Executive Director, Frank Lloyd Wright's Fontana Boathouse, USA

Pedro Guedes, Senior Lecturer in architecture, University of Queensland, Australia

Hasegawa Hideko, INAX Corporation, Tokyo, Japan

Tore Lande Moe, Sunnhordland Museum, Norway

Helen Petersen, Deputy Manager Halsnøy Monastery, Sunnhordland Museum, Norway

Howard Richings, Estates Manager, Royal National Lifeboat Institution, England

Robin Stummer, Society for the Protection of Ancient Buildings, England

Professor Paul Turnbull, Griffith University, Queensland, Australia

Tom Turner, University of Greenwich, England

Delwyn Walker, Waitangi National Trust, New Zealand

PICTURE CREDITS

Every effort has been made to trace all copyright holders. However, the author would like to apologize in advance for any that may have been inadvertently overlooked.

Title page 2–3 David Wall, davidwall.com **Contents page 4–5** Jeanne Apelseth/ SunChaser Productions **Introduction 6–7** Christian Kowalczyk **8–9** Richard White **10–11** Reproduced with the permission of the Sunnhordland Museum, courtesy of Skokloster, Sweden **11** Helen Petersen, Sunnhordland Museum **12 top** Nakazato Katsuhito, from *Topography of Japanese Boathouses*, INAX Publishing **12 bottom left** Library of Congress, Prints and Photographs Division, Historic American Buildings Survey or Historic American Engineering Record, Reproduction Number (HABS FLA,13-MIAM,32A-4) **12 bottom right** Library of Congress, Prints and Photographs Division, Historic American Buildings Survey or Historic American Engineering Record, Reproduction Number (HABS FLA,13-MIAM,32A-6) **13** Nakazato Katsuhito, from *Topography of Japanese Boathouses*, INAX Publishing **14–15** Alasdair Ogilvie **16** © Crown copyright, NMR AA080691 (John Gay) **17** © The British Library **18–19** Alasdair Ogilvie **20–21** Picture Collection, State Library of Victoria **22–3** Courtesy New York Public Library, Astor, Lenox and Tilden Foundations **24** © Crown copyright, NMR AA98_04652 (Eric de Maré) **25** *Illustrated London News*, vol. 17, 1850, p. 477, courtesy of the University of Queensland, Australia **26** *The Civil Engineer and Architect's Journal*, August 1858 (p. 279). RIBA Library **27, 28, 29** Published with the permission of the Société Nationale de Sauvetage en Mer, France **31** Ed Burtynsky

EIGHTEENTH-CENTURY BOATHOUSES
32–3 Alasdair Ogilvie **Botny domik 34** TIPS Images **35** Yury Molodkovets **Traditional South Sea boathouses 36** Courtesy, Prof Paul Turnbull, Griffith University, Australia **38–9** National Library of Australia **Kedleston Hall 40, 41, 42, 43** Alasdair Ogilvie

NINETEENTH-CENTURY BOATHOUSES
44–5 John Frank Nowikowski **Obersee Boathouse 46–7** Christian Kowalczyk **Greenway Boathouse 48, 49** Alasdair Ogilvie **The Dylan Thomas Boathouse 50, 51** Alasdair Ogilvie **Scotney Castle Boathouse 52, 53** © NTPL/David Sellman **Wray Castle Boathouse 54** © The Francis Frith Collection, www.francisfrith.com **55** Alasdair Ogilvie **Haslar Gunboat Yard 56** *Mechanics Magazine*, 3 January 1857, courtesy of Pedro Guedes **Sheerness Boathouse Store 58** Skempton, Professor A. W., 'The Boat Store, Sheerness (1858-60) and its Place in Structural History', *Transactions of the Newcomen Society*, volume XXXII, 1959-60, p. 59 **59 top** © Crown copyright, NMR BB94/20850 (P Williams) **59 bottom** © Crown copyright, NMR AA98/04607 (Eric de Maré) **Victorian Boathouse 60, 61, 62–3** Alasdair Ogilvie **Duke of Portland Boathouse 64–5** © Val Corbett **The Boathouses of Tigre 66–7, 68, 69** John Frank Nowikowski **Boathouse Row 70–71** Sally Weigand **Walmer Lifeboat Station 72–3, 75**

top and bottom John Angerson **74** *The Builder*, 22 May 1875 (pp. 462–3), RIBA Library **Reale Società Canottieri Cerea 76, 77** Images published with the permission of Reale Società Canottieri Cerea **Lodge Park Boathouse 78–9** Alasdair Ogilvie **80 top** Francis Morton catalogue *c.* 1860s, courtesy Pedro Guedes (private collection) **80 bottom** Francis Morton catalogue *c.* 1870s, courtesy Pedro Guedes (private collection) **81** From Boulton & Paul catalogue, *c.*1900 **Clovelly Lifeboat Station 82, 83** Andrew Wheatley

TWENTIETH-CENTURY BOATHOUSES
84–5 © Alvar Aalto Museum **Ryoan-ji Boathouse 86, 87 top and bottom** Adam Mornement **Frank Lloyd Wright's Fontana Boathouse 88, 89** Chuck LaChuisa, courtesy of Frank Lloyd Wright's Fontana Boathouse **90 top** © The Frank Lloyd Wright Fdn, AZ / Art Resource, NY (ART351533) **90 bottom** © The Frank Lloyd Wright Fdn, AZ / Art Resource, NY (ART351532) **91** Chuck LaChuisa, courtesy of Frank Lloyd Wright's Fontana Boathouse **Humboldt Park Boathouse 92, 94, 95** By permission and courtesy of the Chicago Park District Special Collections **92–3** Ron Schramm Photography **Queenscliff Lifeboat Station 96–7** Melanie Ball **97** Queenscliff Historical Society **Noah's Boathouse 98, 99** Illustrations from Sharp and Rendel, *Connell Ward & Lucas*, Frances Lincoln, 2008, pp. 58, 59 **Oxford Boathouses 100–101, 102, 103** Alasdair Ogilvie **Carmel College Boathouse 104** © RCAHMS (Sir Basil Spence Archive), SC 1059575 **105 top** © RCAHMS (Sir Basil Spence Archive), SC 1059570, **105 bottom 106–107** Alasdair Ogilvie **Maori *waka* and *korowai* 108, 109, 110** Karen Knighton **111 top** From a photograph by George Stephenson, courtesy of the Waitangi National Trust **111 bottom** Courtesy of the Waitangi National Trust **'Arc' at Aalto's Experimental House 112–13, 114, 115** © Alvar Aalto Museum; drawings: Courtesy, Claudia Schulz **Northbridge Boatshed 116, 117** Spy Photography (John Doughty); drawings: Courtesy, Design King Co, Sydney

TWENTY-FIRST-CENTURY BOATHOUSES
118–19 Florian Holzherr **Fussach Bootshaus 120, 121 top** Martinez Ignacio **121 bottom, 122 top, 123** Schnabel Albrecht Imanuel; drawings: Courtesy, Marte Marte Architekten **Lake Austin Boat Dock 124, 125, 126, 127** Patrick Wong; drawings: Courtesy Miró Rivera Architects **Minneapolis Rowing Club 128, 129, 130, 131** Mary Luddington and Paul Crosby; drawings: Vincent James Associates Architects **Muskoka Boathouse 132, 135 top, 136 bottom, 137** Ed Burtynsky **133 top, 135 bottom** Bjarke Ingels Group **133 bottom** Howard Sutcliffe **134, 136 top** James Dow **Maritime Youth House 138–9, 139 top** Bjarke Ingels Group **140 bottom, 141** Jens Markus Lindhe **Centre d'Interpretation du Canal 142, 144–5** Didier Boy de la Tour; drawings: Shigeru Ban **Porter Boathouse 146, 147** Paul Crosby; drawing: Vincent James Associates Architects **Tenby Lifeboat Station 148–9, 150, 151** Courtesy of the RNLI **150 bottom** Sue Davies **151** Martin Chambers **Plinio Torno Sports Club 152–3, 154, 155** Beppe Giardino; drawings: MARC Studio **Chesapeake Boathouse 156–9**

Photography by Bob Shimer © Hedrich Blessing, courtesy of Elliott + Associates; drawings: Elliott + Associates **Luna Rossa Team Base 160–61, 162 top, 163** Enrico Cano **162 bottom** sketch by Renzo Piano © RPBW **Floating Boathouse 164–7** Florian Holzherr; drawing: MOS Architects **Louise-Catherine Gallery 168, 169** Shuhei Endo Architect Institute **170–71** Fondation Le Corbusier

INDEX

Aalto, Alvar 84–5, 112–15, 143
Aalto, Elissa 112
ACYC Architects 170
Adam, Robert 40–3
AEG (Allgemeine Elektrizitäts-
    Gesellschaft) 21–4
    Turbinehalle (Berlin, Germany) 21
Akaroa Harbour (New Zealand) *title page*
Alphand, Adolphe 92
aluminium 120–3, 168–9, 170
America's Cup 161, 163
Amersee (Germany) 6–7
'Arc' (Muuratsalo, Finland) 84–5, 112–15
Armstrong-Jones, Anthony, 1st Earl of
    Snowdon 106
art gallery (Carmel College) 104–5, 106

Ban, Shigeru 142–5
Banks, Joseph 37
barge shelter (Pouilly-en-Auxois,
    France) 142–5
barge shelters 142–5, 168–70
bathing house, Greenway (Devon) 48, 49
bath, cold (Kedleston Hall, Derbyshire)
    41, 42, 43
BauerLatoza Studio 95
Bayswater (London), Greek Orthodox
    Cathedral 102
Beaux Arts style 66–7, 71
Beckett (Berkshire) 42
Behrens, Peter 21, 24
Belsize Architects 102, 103
Bentinck, William, 3rd Duke of Portland
    64
Bergen (Norway) 26
Beye, Cudworth 89, 91
Bickford-Smith family 61
BIG (Bjarke Ingels Group) 138–41
Biscayne Bay (Florida) 12
Boat Dock, Lake Austin (Texas) 124–7
Boathouse Row (Philadelphia,
    Pennsylvania) 24–5, 70–1
'boathouse rows' 24–5, 70–1, 156
boating 20–3, 81
boats
    'Laner' boats 46
    Maori canoes 108–11
    rowing shells 156
    Society Island canoes 36, 37, 38–9
    Viking remains 11
    see also lifeboats
Bonino, Michele 77, 152–5
Bordeaux (France) 26
Botik (boat) 35
Botny domik (St Petersburg, Russia)
    34–5
Boulton and Paul 81
Breslau, Louise-Catherine 170
Brest (France) 26
Brown, Lancelot 'Capability' 18
Brutalist style 104–5
budgets 128, 130, 138, 143, 165–6

Buenos Aires Rowing Club 66, 69

Canal de Bourgogne (France) 142–5
canoes
    Maori 108–11
    Society Islands 36, 37, 38–9
Carmel College (Wallingford, Berkshire)
    105, 106
    boathouses 104–7
carvings 108, 109, 110, 111, 116, 117
Castello del Valentino (Turin, Italy) 76, 77
Central Park (New York) 20–1, 22–3
Centre d'Interpretation du Canal
    (Pouilly-en-Auxois, France) 142–5
ceremonial boathouses 13, 108–11
ceremonial canoes 37, 38–9, 108–10
Ceylon (Sri Lanka), Colombo lifeboat
    station 26, 29–30, 73
Chatham Royal Naval Dockyard (Kent)
    26
Cherwell (river) *see* Oxford boathouses
Chesapeake Boathouse (Oklahoma City,
    Oklahoma) 25, 156–9
Chipperfield, David 163
Christ Church boathouse (Oxford) 101,
    102
Christian IV of Denmark 25
Christie, Agatha 48–9, 105
cities, integration of rivers into 24–5,
    156–7
civic landmarks, boathouses as 24–5
Clacton-on-Sea Lifeboat House (Essex)
    30
Clovelly Lifeboat Station (Devon) 82–3
Club Canottieri Italiani (Tigre, Argentina)
    66, 69
Club de Regatas América (Tigre,
    Argentina) 66, 68
Club de Regatas La Marina (Tigre,
    Argentina) 44–5, 66, 66–7
Club Remo Argentino (Tigre, Argentina)
    66, 68
cold bath (Kedleston Hall, Derbyshire)
    41, 42, 43
Colombo lifeboat station (Sri Lanka) 26,
    29–30, 73
Colonial Revival style 70
Como, Lake (Italy) 152–5
compressed paper tubes 30, 142–5
concrete 104–5, 106, 147, 151
    reinforced 26, 88–91, 89, 98–9
Connell, Amyas 99
Constance, Lake 120–2
Cook, First Lieutenant (later Captain)
    James 37
Cooke, Charles 26, 72–3, 74, 82
Coonley kindergarten project (Riverside,
    Illinois) 91
Copenhagen (Denmark), Royal
    Boathouse 25
Corpus Christi and St John's boathouse
    (Oxford) 101–2, 103

corrugated iron 25, 57
    kit buildings 78–81
corrugated sheet metal 148, 150
Courtin, John 91
Cowan, Dr 51
'cribs' 133, 135
Crimean War (1853–6) 57, 58
Curzon, Sir Nathaniel (later 1st Baron
    Scarsdale) 41, 42

Darwin D Martin House (Buffalo, New
    York State) 91
davits, for boat storage *contents page* 9,
    30, 97
Dawson, Dr James 54
de Maré, Eric 58, 59
Dead Man's Folly (Christie, 1956) 48–9
defence *see* naval boathouses; naval
    fleets
Denne of Deal, Messrs 75
Deptford Royal Naval Dockyard (London)
    25, 26
development, restrictions on 9, 30, 70–1,
    116
Devoke Water (Cumbria) 14–15
dockyards, British naval 25–6
Douglass, W T 82–3
dry rot 25
Dubuis, Oscar F 94
Duke of Portland Boathouse (Ullswater,
    Cumbria) 11, 64–5
Dunkirk (France), lifeboat station 27
Dutton, John 'Crump' 81
Dylan Thomas Boathouse (Laugharne,
    Carmarthenshire, Wales) 50–1

East Anglian boathouses 17
Elektra Rowing Club 24
Elliott, Rand 156–9
Elton, Edward 49
Elton, James Marwood 49
Emes, William 41
Endeavour (James Cook's ship) 37
Endo, Shuhei 168–9, 170
Englischer Garten (Munich, Germany)
    21
English landscape style 18–20, 21, 40–1
Enville Hall (Staffordshire) 42
environmental impacts of boathouses 9,
    30, 125, 164–5
Erling Skakke (Erling the Wry) 11
Erquy (France), lifeboat station 29
Etruria (Staffordshire) 20
Experimental House (Muuratsalo,
    Finland) 112, 115
eye catchers 13, 18

Fairmount Park (Philadelphia,
    Pennsylvania) 24–5, 70–1
Féderation International du Sport
    d'Aviron (International Rowing
    Federation) 76

Federazione Italiana di Canottaggio
    (Italian Rowing Federation) 76
fishing 12, 13
Fishing Room and Boathouse, Kedleston
    Hall (Derbyshire) 32–3, 40–3
fishing rooms 32–3, 40–2, 42
Fishing Temple (Beresford Dale,
    Derbyshire) 42
fleets
    boathouses for 25–6, 56, 57
    fishing fleets 13
    naval fleets 13, 25–6, 35, 57
Floating Asylum (*Louise-Catherine*)
    168–70, 170–1
Floating Boathouse (Lake Huron,
    Canada) 30, 118–19, 164–7
Fontana Boathouse (Buffalo, New York
    State) 88–91, 143
Fontana, Tom 91
foundations 65, 112, 133, 135
France 26, 29
    see also Centre d'Interpretation du
    Canal; Louise-Catherine Gallery
Frank Lloyd Wright's Rowing Boathouse
    Corporation 89, 91
French Salvation Army 168–70
Furness, Frank 71
Fussach Bootshaus (Fussach, Austria)
    120–3

Gagey, Jean 29
Galejhus (Royal Boathouse),
    Copenhagen (Denmark) 25
Garden, Hugh Mackie Gordon 95
Germany 20, 26, 29
    see also AEG; Amersee; Obersee
Gilpin, William Sawrey 53
Gottlieb, Julius 104, 105, 106
Gottlieb, Lt Commander E J 106
Gower, Lady Victoria Levenson 73
Gravelines (France), lifeboat station 28
Great Northern War (1700–21) 35
Greek Orthodox Cathedral (Bayswater,
    London) 102
Greene, Colonel Godfrey Thomas 58–9
Greenway (Devon) 48–9
Grenald, Raymond 70–1, 71
Group of Seven 133

habitat disturbance 9, 30
Hafrsfjord (Norway) *contents page*
Halsnøy Kloster (Norway) 9–11
Hancock, Thomas 106
Haslar Gunboat Yard (Gosport,
    Hampshire) 56–7
Haussmann, Georges-Eugène (Baron
    Haussmann) 92
Hennigsdorf (Germany) 24
Herangi, Princess Te Puea 108
Hill Top (Sawrey, Cumbria) 54
Hitchcock, Henry-Russell 91
Hoopers Bay (New Zealand) 8–9

Horner, H P 54
Humboldt Park Boathouse (Chicago) 92–5
Hussey, Edward (III) 53

Ine (Japan) 12
International Exhibition (London, 1862) 80, 81
International Rowing Federation (Féderation International du Sport d'Aviron) 76
iron, corrugated 25, 57, 78–81
Isis (river) see Oxford boathouses
Italian Rowing Federation (Federazione Italiana di Canottaggio) 76

James, Vincent 128–9, 146–7
Japonisme 81
Jenney, William Le Baron 92–4
Jensen, Jens 94
Juler, Mary Anderson 99
Jyvässkylä (Finland) 112

karesansui (dry landscape garden), Ryoan-ji (Japan) 86
Kedleston Hall (Derbyshire), Fishing Room and Boathouse 20, 32–3, 40–3
KEE Architecture Inc 147
Keroman Submarine Base (Lorient, France) 26
Kevlar 156, 160–3
King, Jon 116–17
korowai (waka shelter) 108–11
Krolmark, Anne-Mette 84–5, 112–15
Kupe (Maori ancestor) 110, 111

La Pallice (France) 26
Lake Austin Boat Dock (Austin, Texas) 124–7
Lake District (Cumbria) 16
    see also Devoke Water; Duke of Portland Boathouse
landscape style 18–20, 21, 40–1
'Laner' boats 46
Larkin Administration Building (Buffalo, New York State) 89
launching lifeboats 27, 28, 29, 30, 82, 148, 150
    launching tractors 75, 82, 83
Le Corbusier (Charles-Edouard Jeanneret-Gris) 170
LED lights 70–1
Libeskind, Daniel 25
lifeboat stations 13, 26–30
    Clovelly (Devon) 82–3
    Colombo (Sri Lanka) 26, 29–30, 73
    Queenscliff (Australia) 96–7
    Tenby (Wales) 148–51
    Walmer (Kent) 72–5
    see also RNLI
lifeboats 13, 26–30, 75, 82–3, 97, 148, 150, 151
    davit-hung 30, 97
    launching 27, 28, 29, 30, 82, 148, 150
    see also lifeboat stations; RNLI
lifesaving technology 13, 29, 148
lighting, Boathouse Row (Philadelphia) 70–1

Lodge Park (Gloucestershire) 78–81
Loeb Boathouse, Central Park (New York) 20–1
Loeb, Carl M 20–1
Lorient (France) 26
Louise-Catherine (barge) 168–71
Louise-Catherine Gallery (Paris) 168–71
Lowther, Sir James, 1st Earl of Lonsdale 64
Lucas, Colin 98–9
Lucas, Lloyd and Co. 98–9
Lucas, Ralph 99
Luna Rossa (boat) 163
Luna Rossa Team Base (Valencia, Spain) 160–3

maintenance 9, 87
Mallowan, Max 49
Mandarin Duck Pond (Kyoyochi), Ryoan-ji (Japan) 86–7
Manyana Boat Dock (Lake Austin, Texas) 125
Maori boathouses 108–11
Maori boats 108–11
MARC Studio 77
Maritime Youth House (Sundby Harbour, Denmark) 138–41
Marks, Ted 91
Marte, Stefan and Bernhard 120–3
Martin, Edgar 95
mausolea, boathouses as 13, 34–5, 112–15
Mechanics' Magazine 56, 57
Melanesia 36–9
Melbourne (Australia), 'boathouse row' 25
Menier Factory (France) 58
Meredith, Michael 118–19, 164–7
Merton boathouse (Oxford) 101
Messrs Denne of Deal 75
Meyers, Jay 91
military boathouses 13, 24, 25–6, 56–7, 58–9
Minneapolis Rowing Club (Minnesota) 128–31
Miró, Juan 124–7
Miró Rivera Architects 124–7
Modern Movement 21, 58, 91, 98–9
Mongewell (Berkshire) see Carmel College
Morton, Francis 80, 81
MOS Architects 118–19, 164–7
Moscow (Russia) 35
Mousetrap, The (Christie, 1952) 105
Mukerjee, Subhash 152–5
Munich (Germany), Englischer Garten 21
Munrow, Ralph M 12
Music Court and pavilion, Humboldt Park (Chicago) 94, 95
Muskoka Boathouse (Ontario, Canada) 31, 132–7

Nash, John 18
National Institution for the Preservation of Life from Shipwreck (later RNLI) 29
naval boathouses 13, 24, 25–6, 56–7,

58–9
naval fleets 13, 26, 35, 56, 57
Nemo Propheta in Patria (boat) 112–15
New Zealand 29, 37, 110, 111
    see also Akaroa Harbour; Hoopers Bay; Robinson's Bay; waka shelter
Ngatokimatawhaorua (Maori ceremonial war canoe) 108–10, 111
Noah's Boathouse (Buckinghamshire) 98–9
Noah's House (Buckinghamshire) 99
Norfolk Broads (East Anglia) 17
Northbridge Boatshed (Sydney, Australia) 116–17
Northumberland, 4th Duke of see Percy, Algernon
Norway 26
    see also Hafrsfjord; Halsnøy Kloster
Nukutawhiti (Maori ancestor) 110, 111

oars 110, 111
    as inspiration 102, 103, 128, 129
    representations of 157, 158, 159
Oberschöneweide boathouse (Germany) 24
Obersee boathouse (Germany) 11, 46–7
Oki (Japan) 13
Oklahoma City Boathouse Foundation 156
Oklahoma City (Oklahoma) 25, 156–7
Olmsted, Frederick Law 20, 92
OUB (Oxford University Boathouse) 102, 106
Oxford boathouses 100–3

Page, William 110, 111
paper tubes (recycled) 30, 142–5
Paris 92
    see also Louise-Catherine Gallery
Parkinson, Sydney 36–9
parks 13, 18, 20–1, 70–1, 92–5
Pembroke Royal Naval Dockyard (Pembrokeshire) 26
Percy, Algernon, 4th Duke of Northumberland 29
Peter the Great 35
Peter-Paul Fortress (St Petersburg, Russia) 34–5
Philadelphia (Pennsylvania), Boathouse Row 24–5, 70–1
Piano, Renzo 160–3
Picturesque Revival style 53
Picturesque Victorian style 70
piers 96–7
piles, use of 37, 53, 61, 138–41, 148–51
planning restrictions 77, 120, 128
plastic sheeting (ribbed) 142–5
Plexiglass 152–5
Plinio Torno Sports Club (Lake Como, Italy) 152–5
Polignac, Princess Singer de 170
polycarbonate 156–9, 160–3
Polynesian voyages to New Zealand 110, 111
pontoons
    boathouse on 118–19, 164–7
    Louise-Catherine barge 168–9, 170
Port Phillip Pilots 97

Porter Boathouse (University of Wisconsin, Madison) 146–7
Portsmouth Royal Naval Dockyard (Hampshire) 24, 26
Potter, Beatrix 54
Pouilly-en-Auxois (France) 143
Prairie Style 89, 92–5
prefabricated buildings 78–81
profiled aluminium sheeting 168–9, 170
public parks 13, 18, 20–1, 70–1, 92–5
Puttnam, Anthony 91

Queenscliff lifeboat station (Australia) 96–7
Queenscliffe (lifeboat) 97

Rawnsley, Canon Hardwicke 54
Reale Società Canottieri Cerea (Turin, Italy) 76–7, 154
recycled Kevlar sails 160–3
recycled paper tubes 30, 142–5
recycling of boathouse sites 9–11, 30, 46, 64, 65, 82, 86, 117
reinforced concrete 26, 88–91, 89, 98–9
repairs 9, 87
Repton, Humphry 18, 49
Repton, John Adey 18
restrictions on development 9, 30, 70–1, 116
ribbed plastic sheeting 142–5
Ringstetten boathouse (Philadelphia, Pennsylvania) 71
Rivera, Miguel 124–7
rivers, integration into cities 24–5, 156–7
RNLB Florence 148
RNLB John R Webb 151
RNLB Spirit of Clovelly 82, 83
RNLI (Royal National Lifeboat Institution) 26, 29–30, 82
    see also lifeboat stations; lifeboats
Robinson's Bay (Akaroa Harbour, New Zealand) title page
Romanov, Nikita Ivanovich 35
Rosen, Rabbi Kopul 105
rowing 13, 21, 152
rowing clubs 13, 66–9, 70–1, 76–7, 128–31, 152
rowing shells, as inspiration 156–9
Royal Boathouse (Galejhus), Copenhagen (Denmark) 25
Royal Dockyards (Britain) 24, 25–6
Royal National Lifeboat Institution see RNLI
Russia 20, 57
    see also Botny domik
Ryoan-ji boathouse (Kyoto, Japan) 11, 86–7

Sackville-West, Lionel 66, 69
sails, recycled 160–3
Saint-Nazaire (France) 26
Salvation Army (France) 168–70, 170–1
Salvin, Anthony 53
Sample, Hilary 118–19, 164–7
Scarsdale, Lord see Curzon, Sir Nathaniel
Schmidt, Richard 95
Schuylkill Navy 71

Schuylkill River (Philadelphia, Pennsylvania) 24–5, 70–1
Scotney Castle boathouse (Kent) 52–3
Scotney New Castle (Kent) 53
Scott, John Oldrid 102
sculls, as inspiration 156–9
Sculz, Claudia 84–5, 112–15
Sheerness Boat Store (Kent) 58–9
sheet metal 168–9, 170
shells (rowing shells), as inspiration 156–9
Shim, Brigitte 31, 132–7
Shingle Style 70, 147
Shipwrecked Fishermen and Mariners' Benevolent Society 148
Silver Skiff Regatta 76, 77
Simons, Chaim 106
sites 9, 30, 165–6
    recycling of 9–11, 30, 46, 64, 65, 82, 86, 117
skating 95
slipways 49, 56, 57, 65
    for lifeboats 27, 28, 29, 30, 82, 83, 96, 97, 148, 150, 151
Snowdon, Earl of see Armstrong-Jones, Anthony
Society Islands 36–9
South Sea boathouses 36–9
Spence, Sir Basil 104–5, 106
Speyers, John 18

Sri Lanka (Ceylon), Colombo lifeboat station 26, 29–30, 73
stave construction 11
Stourhead (Wiltshire) 18
Sullivan, Louis 94, 95
Sutcliffe, Howard 31, 132–7

Tahiti 36–9
Tale of Peter Rabbit, The (Beatrix Potter, 1902) 54
Team Alinghi 163
Tenby lifeboat stations (Pembrokeshire, Wales) 148–51
terraces 120, 121, 163
Terragni, Attilio and Carlo 152
Thames, River 100–3, 105
Thomas, Caitlin 51
Thomas, Dylan 51
Tigre (Argentina) 44–5, 66–9
tiles 24, 30
translucent materials 153–5, 156, 157–8, 160–3
Trent and Mersey Canal 20
Trevarno boathouse (Cornwall) 60–3
Trinity boathouse (Oxford) 101
Trondheim (Norway) 26

U-boat pens and bunkers 26
Ullswater (Cumbria), Duke of Portland Boathouse 11

Under Milk Wood (Thomas, 1954) 51
Unity Church (Oak Park, Illinois) 91
University College Boathouse (Oxford) 102, 103, 106
University of Wisconsin Boat Club 89–91, 146–7
University of Wisconsin (Madison, Wisconsin), Porter Boathouse 146–7
urban areas, integration of rivers into 24–5, 156–7
urban boathouses 20–5
urban expansion 13
urban regeneration 156

Vaux, Calvert 20, 22–3
Veles e Vents spectator building (Valencia, Spain) 163
Victoria (Australia) 96–7
Victorian boathouse (Trevarno, Cornwall) 60–3
Victorian Gothic style 70
Vikings 11
Vist, Alexander 34–5
volksparks 21

Wadham, St Anne's and St Hugh's boathouse (Oxford) 101
Waitangi (New Zealand) 108, 109–10, 111
    Treaty of (1840) 108, 111

waka shelter (korowai) 108–11
waka taua (Maori war canoes) 108–11
Walmer Lifeboat Station (Kent) 72–5
Walton, Izaak 42
war canoes (waka taua) 108–11
Ward, Basil 99
Wasmuth Portfolio (Frank Lloyd Wright, 1910/11) 90, 91
Wedgwood, Josiah 20
West Side Rowing Club 88–91
White, Thomas 56–7
Woodchester Park (Gloucestershire) 18–19
Woolwich Royal Naval Dockyard 26
Wordsworth, William 54
World War II (1939–45) 26
Wray Castle boathouse (Cumbria) 54–5
Wright, Frank Lloyd 88–91, 94, 95, 147
writing rooms 13, 48–9, 51
Wroxham Broad (East Anglia), boathouse 17

yacht club, Sundby Harbour (Denmark) 138–41
Yahara River (Wisconsin) 89, 91
youth club, Sundby Harbour (Denmark) 138–41

Zillhardt, Madeleine 170

Frances Lincoln Limited
4 Torriano Mews
Torriano Avenue
London NW5 2RZ
www.franceslincoln.com

Boathouses
Copyright © Frances Lincoln Limited 2010
Text copyright © Adam Mornement 2010
Illustrations copyright © as listed on page 173
Quotation on page 48 AGATHA CHRISTIE ® POIROT ® Dead Man's Folly copyright
© 1956 Agatha Christie Limited (a Chorion company). All rights reserved.

First Frances Lincoln edition 2010

A catalogue record for this book is available from the British Library.

978-0-7112-2868-9

Printed and bound in China

1 2 3 4 5 6 7 8 9

Commissioned and edited by Jane Crawley